A FOOT IN THE DOOR

A FOOT IN THE DOOR

NETWORKING YOUR WAY
INTO THE HIDDEN JOB MARKET

Katharine Hansen

TEN SPEED PRESS
BERKELEY TORONTO

This book is dedicated to Theodore Stewart Fries Jr., a very special young man whom I am proud to claim as a member of my personal network.

I would like to thank Dr. Rebecca Oliphant for suggesting informational interviews as an assignment for my class.

Thanks to Keefe Karvaski for his research assistance.

I thank the many members of the National Association of Colleges and Employers (NACE) and members of NACE's Jobplace on-line discussion group for sharing their survey responses, stories, comments, and wisdom. Thanks also to Michael Kaplan and Jennifer Sumner.

As always, I thank my students at Stetson University who inspire my writing. I especially thank Nicole Zimmerman, Nathan Moro, Mark Siviter, Dawn Baldock, Lauren Hensley, Scooter Cardoza, Stacy Williams, Kyle Jackson, Crystal Coons, Bryan Sands, Kelley Dewey, Holly Haroff, Mike Gunning, Steven Cervino, Paul Harris, Lupe Cuevas, Heidi Lozano, Patrick Hartnett, Damon Mitrakos, Jennifer Guidish, Christopher Maffett, and Lisa Marsh.

And thanks and love always, of course, to RSH.

For up-to-date information about networking, please visit:
http://www.quintcareers.com/

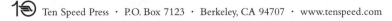

Ten Speed Press · P.O. Box 7123 · Berkeley, CA 94707 · www.tenspeed.com

Distributed in Australia by Simon and Schuster Australia; in Canada by Ten Speed Press Canada; in New Zealand by Southern Publishers Group; in South Africa by Real Books; in the United Kingdom and Europe by Airlift Books; and in Southeast Asia by Berkeley Books.

Text and cover design by Paul Kepple @ Headcase Design

Library of Congress Cataloging-in-Publication Data on file with the publisher.

First printing, 2000
Printed in Canada

1 2 3 4 5 6 7 8 9 10 — 04 03 02 01 00

650.14
Han
57878

TABLE OF CONTENTS

INTRODUCTION

I did my first real networking in the early 1980s in the form of informational interviewing. I had learned about the concept from Richard Nelson Bolles's *What Color Is Your Parachute?*, which was already a classic in the career field and has since gone on to even greater success and recognition.

It was when, as a college instructor, I began to teach my business communication students about networking and assigned them to conduct informational interviews that I truly began to see the power of networking. My partner, Randall Hansen, and I have demonstrated our commitment to the written tools of job seeking in our earlier books, *Dynamic Cover Letters* and *Dynamic Cover Letters for New Graduates*. I remain committed to the importance of the written word to career success, but I'm well aware that the past two decades have brought a sea change in job seeking. Perhaps as a coping mechanism in the face of a constantly changing technological and global economy, the importance of building relationships has come to the fore in every area from marketing to politics. Job hunting is no different. Relationships are everything, and to form relationships, you have to network.

I got especially excited when I observed my students putting into practice what I had taught them about networking. They were blown away by their success with networking and informational interviewing. They used these tools to affirm career choices, avoid inappropriate options, try on careers, gain valuable insider information—and most importantly, make contacts. Most students attained a solid network of contacts and insider information that enabled them by graduation time to approach employers with a clear advantage over other job seekers. Several students every semester received internship and job offers as a direct result of their networking and informational interviews. In short, networking can be a life-changing activity. It is my hope that this book will guide readers through this invaluable process.

This book is designed to give you lots of ideas about where and with whom to network. I surveyed 123 career counselors and others to learn about their networking experiences and ideas—and they contributed generously and abundantly. *A Foot in the Door* guides you through the process and over the obstacles of networking. The informational interviewing section is intended to be the most comprehensive resource available on how to conduct an informational interview. The book provides numerous networking tips you may not have thought of and testimonials from successful networkers. It touches on the special needs of underrepresented groups and the importance of follow-up. Look for the special "Foot" notes at the bottom of many pages for even more information.

Please consider me a member of your personal network. People in your network should provide you with advice and support. I offer you both in *A Foot in the Door.* I wish you much success as you build your network.

—*Katharine Hansen*

PART·ONE

NETWORKING:

WHAT, WHY, HOW, WHO, WHERE, AND WHEN

Chapter One

WHAT IS NETWORKING?

IT'S ALL ABOUT RELATIONSHIP BUILDING

Early in the popular 1996 film *Jerry Maguire*, the title character, hating the sleazy and uncaring sports agent he has become, harkens back to the words of his mentor, Dickie Fox, who had proclaimed that their business was "all about personal relationships." Some people are as turned off by networking as they are by sports agents because networking seems so similar to sales and marketing. Well, networking is a lot like sales and marketing, and all three are about establishing and cultivating personal relationships. Maybe you're uncomfortable with the idea of marketing and selling yourself. But you're probably a lot more comfortable with the idea of making friends and of talking to people. That's what networking comes down to: talking to people, making friends, building relationships—all with a little self-promotion and sales savvy thrown in. "Before it was called networking, it was just being friendly and interested in people," observes Nelson Barnett, director of the Lyon College Career Development Center. When one of your contacts has some promising career information to impart, the first person he or she will want to tell is a friend—you, if you've successfully built the relationship.

Networking doesn't mean asking everyone you run into if he or she knows where the job openings are. It means establishing relationships so that you can enlist support and comfortably ask for ideas, advice, and referrals to those with hiring power.

Leslie Smith of the National Association of Female Executives defines networking as the process of "planning and making contacts and sharing information for professional and personal gain." The key word is "sharing." Many individuals are uncomfortable with the notion of networking because it feels like "using" people. Successful networking doesn't mean milking your contacts for all they're worth; it means participating in a give-and-take. Networking is at its most effective when both the networker and the contact benefit from the relationship. Even if your contact does not benefit immediately from knowing you, he or she should gain something from the relationship eventually.

We've all heard the old expression: "It's not what you know; it's who you know." The suggestion is that no matter how smart and talented you are, you don't have the same competitive edge in the job market as someone who is well connected with the people who possess hiring power. There is some truth in that adage. Networking is the process through which you get connected and build relationships with people who can help advance your career. Not everyone you encounter in the networking process has hiring power; in fact, most members of your network probably will not have hiring power. These intermediaries give you valuable information and career advice while steering you toward opportunities and the honchos who do hire. They make it possible for you to connect with those with hiring power for this reason: You are always more likely to be considered by a hiring manager if you are referred by a mutual acquaintance than if you tried to approach the hiring manager "cold."

Do you already have to know a lot of people to be able to network effectively? Absolutely not. All you have to do is want to know more people than you already do, people who can assist you in your quest for your ideal job. You should also be willing to do as much as you can to encourage others to want to get to know you and help you. It takes only one person to start your network, because that person can refer you to others. If each new person you contact does the same, your network will expand exponentially.

FOOT NOTE

If you're attending a networking event, don't forget to take a pen. You'll get most of your information by exchanging business cards, but you'll occasionally encounter someone without cards or you will wish to jot down information not found on a business card.

Some of the most successful people network. A consummate politician, President Bill Clinton is said to have maintained an index-card system containing the names of everyone he had met since college. For folks like Clinton, networking is more than a job-hunting technique trotted out when needed; it's a way of life. The most successful networkers make it a lifestyle, but you can benefit from networking even if you don't do it all the time.

Networking is viewed as even more important than such hallowed job-hunting tools as resumes. Professional resume writer Susan Britton Whitcomb, author of *Resume Magic*, suggests that a resume is not at its most effective when it precedes your interview with a hiring manager. "A better strategy," Whitcomb writes, "is to establish rapport with the hiring manager before submitting a resume. For most people, an initial face-to-face or voice contact is more engaging than print-on-paper."

Your goal should be to form relationships that are so powerful that your contacts feel invested in your success—and you in theirs. On his CareerLab Web site (*http://www.careerlab.com/*), William S. Frank recalls a successful job hunter he once met who said, "I create relationships. The relationships create jobs."

College career counselor Tracy Hakala tells a story of how building and maintaining relationships paid off for a candidate her office hired:

> A [career services] colleague at another university was interested in visiting other career services offices while she was visiting family on holiday. She was very professional in contacting [our office], making arrangements and in visiting us. At this point we had no position openings, nor did this person indicate that she was looking for different employment. She later made it a point to talk to our director at a professional association conference. Plus she kept in contact with me through e-mail. When she saw that we had a position opening a few months later, she indicated her interest, applied, and was eventually offered the position. It really did make a difference when her application came around. We already knew a little about her and had been impressed with her professionalism. I think it gave her an edge over the other candidates.

Finding a job is far from the only reason for networking; as placement counselor Judy Robinson points out, "Networking not only assists you in finding available positions in the field; it also provides you with the opportunity to learn more about the profession and gain insights into trends in the industry that can be helpful in the interviewing process." Career specialist Robin Hammond comments, "I find that my greatest professional growth recently has occurred as the result of networking, and not as a result of my professional work."

Before moving further in our discussion, it will be useful to look at two types of networking and how they fit into the overall process. At its most basic level, networking can be divided into two categories:

- **Developmental networking:** Networking for further contacts and referrals
- **Strategic networking:** Direct networking that lays the foundation for hiring

Considerable overlap can occur between these categories, but if you want to determine the best way to make contact, it pays to have a sense of the kind of networking you're doing.

Let's look at some scenarios and how they fit these categories.

Leslie, a college junior, was concerned about getting a job upon graduation. She initiated developmental networking by speaking with her immediate family and friends to ask them for ideas about employers she might approach and other people she might contact. Her networking paid off, resulting in dozens of suggestions. She then embarked on strategic networking by contacting some of the employers and set up informational interviews, which proved highly effective (see Part 3). Some of the referrals she received were not people with hiring power but were contacts whom Leslie could add to her network. She phoned, wrote to, or e-mailed many of the

FOOT NOTE

As you prepare to network for the first time, pump up your self-esteem as much as possible. Confidence will help make you a successful networker, and a healthy ego can provide a suit of armor to shield you from the occasional rebuffs you will inevitably encounter.

people who had been referred to her, and as a result she obtained more ideas, more names, and more suggestions of employers with whom to conduct informational interviews. Thus she repeated the cycle that started with developmental networking and led to strategic networking.

John decided that he was burned out on his job as a systems analyst and decided he was ready for a change. He wanted to make a major career shift, but he did not know many people in the field he was considering. For him, developmental networking started with joining a professional association for his new field and attending a social event specifically geared toward networking. He made the rounds at the event, introducing himself to many members and exchanging business cards with them. Armed with many new contacts, he began to phone his new acquaintances for lengthier conversations. Some of the phone conversations were just that—chats on the phone—but John's contacts usually gave him useful information and additional referrals. Other people that John called suggested they meet for lunch or that John come to see them in their offices. Those strategic networking meetings, too, resulted in more referrals and solid leads.

Katrina liked her job but felt she was stagnating and not advancing. She wanted to stay in her field but felt career progress might be faster with a different company. Unfortunately, her job kept her almost too busy to attend events where she might network. She was also somewhat shy and not totally comfortable with the idea of networking. Katrina was, however, a member of several Internet on-line discussion groups, which served as her venue for developmental networking. She also joined a networking group on the Internet that gave her names of others in her field. Through her "virtual" conversations with her on-line colleagues, Katrina learned of several job possibilities, got the names of a number of contacts, and obtained some valuable advice that propelled her toward strategic networking and learning how to break in at one of her dream companies.

If we were to outline the process that Leslie, John, and Katrina each followed to some extent, the plan might look like this:

DEVELOPMENTAL NETWORKING

• Begin constructing network by compiling a list of possible contacts.

• Strategize how you will connect with these people—in person, letter, e-mail, or phone. See Chapter 3.

• Expand your network and prepare for strategic networking by asking contacts for advice and especially referrals.

• Follow up with your initial contacts with thanks and progress reports.

STRATEGIC NETWORKING

• Arrange meetings and informational interviews with these second-tier contacts your network has referred you to. These new contacts will likely be in a better position than your initial contacts to propel you toward being hired.

• Solicit additional referrals from your second-tier contacts.

• Maintain contact with all promising members of your network, continually updating and thanking them, while seeking new advice and referrals.

• Once you've landed that job, tell your contacts the good news. Continue to maintain relationships with preemployment network while adding new contacts from your new workplace.

Chapter Two

WHY IS NETWORKING SO IMPORTANT?

THE HIDDEN JOB MARKET—THE 75 TO 95 PERCENT OF JOBS THAT ARE NEVER ADVERTISED

What's the average person's image of the traditional job-hunting process? Perhaps responding to want ads and sending out a lot of resumes "cold" to likely employers? Most of us know enough about how the job market has changed to realize that such an image is rather antiquated. We know that the job seeker who answers ads, makes cold contacts with employers, and then sits back to wait for results will probably have a long wait indeed. Networking has been touted as a vital part of the mix for close to two decades now; in fact, in one recent survey 87 percent of respondents said networking is an important resource when looking for a new job. Others assert that networking ability affects the length and ease of the job search; Michael Broscio, in an article in *Healthcare Financial Management* magazine, listed networking among the top ten variables affecting job-search success. But how many of us know why networking is so important and why the traditional methods are no longer enough?

It's because the vast majority of job vacancies—estimates range from 75 to 95 percent—are hidden from the average job seeker. These positions are never advertised and are part of the "hidden" or "closed" job market. You can find out about these jobs only through word of mouth, and word of mouth means networking.

The U.S. Department of Labor, following interviews with several thousand newly hired employees, recently summarized how people get their jobs:

- 24 percent from direct contact with potential employers ("cold" contacts)
- 23 percent from school or alumni placement offices, employment or temporary services

- 5 percent from responding to classified advertising
- 48 percent from referrals from friends or relatives (networking)

And there you have it: Almost half of all jobs come from networking!

The kinds of jobs that are advertised are probably not the ones you want. They tend to be the most competitive, yet lowest-level and poorest-paying positions. The best jobs at the highest levels with top salaries are rarely advertised. They are most likely ferreted out through networking.

WHY MOST EMPLOYERS *DON'T* ADVERTISE

Employers' reluctance to advertise is partly tied to the economy. The years approaching the twenty-first century have seen very low unemployment numbers in the United States. With the vast majority of the adult population employed, employers assume not many prospective workers will be scanning the want ads. With a limited audience for their ads, employers are disinclined to spend money on advertising for workers.

The second reason is more psychological. The people who read want ads are looking for jobs. While it might seem that an employer offering jobs and people looking for jobs are a perfect match, that's not often the case in the employer's mind. The employer has to wonder, Why is this person looking for a job? The answer that pops into the employer's head, whether fairly or not, is probably not a positive one. People look for jobs, many employers believe, because they are unhappy losers, job-hoppers, or unproductive malcontents who blame poor performance on their employers and believe switching jobs will solve their problems. Employers would rather go after people who aren't necessarily looking for work. In the employer's mind, those people will be successful, productive contributors to the company's bottom line.

Employers also know that the best candidates are likely to be those referred to them through word of mouth. It is only when employers are truly desperate to fill an opening that they place an ad.

"The last place I want to pull applicants from is the classified ads of major newspapers," observes Ohio State University career counselor B. J. O'Bruba. "Classified ad applicants are unreferred, untested, and unknown. The first place I look for applicants is within my current or previous organizations or applicants who were referred to me by professional colleagues and acquaintances. These applicants are better referenced, tested, and known." Peggy Killian, director of Career Services at Elmhurst College, agrees, "I have discovered through experience that I will hire only people I know through networking."

Further, busy employers simply don't have the time to go through the mountains of resumes a classified ad is likely to produce. Employers often find it far more efficient to ask members of their personal networks to refer high-quality candidates to them.

Finally, the process of defining job vacancies can take a long time. In some companies, a year or more can elapse between initial conceptualization of a job and actually filling the position. Thus, at any given time, theoretical positions may exist within an organization, but the formal mechanisms of funding, structuring, and writing a job description for the position mean that the job cannot yet be advertised. That's another reason networking is so valuable. If you can tap into a job in its embryonic stages, you will have a huge advantage over those who wait to answer ads. Let's say Megabucks Corporation is planning a position that you're well qualified for, but the firm is six months away from advertising the job. You don't know about the position, but your networking efforts lead you to a key person, Joe Honcho, at Megabucks. After talking with you, Honcho attends a meeting and tells his colleagues, "Hey, I just met someone who would be great for that position we're working on." The management team may even decide to reshape the job to fit your unique qualifications. With his team's blessing, Honcho gets you in for a series of interviews. Megabucks still may not be able to hire you until all the t's are crossed and the i's dotted, but once the job is official, you are in—all before Megabucks even had the chance to advertise the position.

 FOOT NOTE

"Networking is the way to go for not-so-obvious occupations," observes engineering placement recruiter DeLynn Davenport. "I am a recruiter, but I am looking for a position which will make use of my French degree (that isn't teaching or translating). I have gotten quite a few leads from my co-workers and people who work for international companies and government agencies."

Chapter Three

HOW TO MAKE CONTACT

Part 2 details how to network once you've made contact, but here we examine ways to make initial contact.

IN PERSON

In-person networking generally occurs at two different stages of the networking process. You may talk with folks face-to-face when you are initially seeking referrals and ideas, as Leslie from Chapter 1 did with her circle of friends and John did at the networking event he attended. The second stage occurs when those contacts lead to face-to-face meetings (lunches, informational interviews) with the people you're referred to, usually after an interim step in which you call, write, or e-mail these referrals. Numerous venues for making in-person contact are suggested throughout this book, especially in Chapter 5. Once you've been referred to new prospective network contacts, you have to decide how you will contact them.

MAIL

A well-written letter is probably the best route when you are contacting someone you've been referred to but don't know at all, or when you contact someone "cold." It's a fine way to introduce yourself and state in an eloquent way your reason for contacting the recipient. Many people are more comfortable with a letter because it is less intrusive than "cold calling," and you don't have to worry about playing "telephone tag," or about getting past a "gatekeeping" secretary, receptionist, or assistant. Bear in mind that if you write a letter (a sample appears in Chapter 12), you will still have to follow up with a phone call. You never want to place the burden of contacting you on the person you've written to. While it's perfectly possible that the recipient will pick up the phone and call you soon after receiving your letter, you should not write your letter as though you expect that scenario to occur. Also realize that every piece of mail in a person's in-box represents a task that must be handled (even if the task is simply tossing the letter in the trash). Make your letter as concise and to-the-point as possible.

E-MAIL

E-mail is often a good choice when you are acquainted with the recipient or when you know a company's culture is oriented toward e-mail, as technology companies are. People who are accustomed to communicating through e-mail will respond well to this method. E-mail is also a reasonable choice because it's more immediate than a letter, yet less intrusive than a phone call; the recipient can read and respond at her own convenience. The text of the sample letter in Chapter 12 is equally applicable to e-mail messages, which are essentially letters without the business-letter trappings. As with a letter, you should not leave the ball in the recipient's court, but with the ease of responding to e-mail, your recipient is more likely to respond to e-mail than to a letter. The response, however, may well be "Call me."

PHONE

If the rule is never to leave the ball in the recipient's court, it's clear that most networking roads ultimately lead to a phone call. If you loathe writing letters but are completely at ease on the phone, you may prefer the phone as your initial point of contact. Pitfalls include the inevitable "phone tag" of the business world and the possibility of catching your contact off guard. Persistence and politeness are keys to overcoming these obstacles.

The phone call is an essential tool in networking, so if you are uncomfortable making calls, you will most likely need to confront your fears and make yourself pick up the phone. The more you do it, the easier it will get. Practice your networking phone conversation technique on your friends. Sample phone scripts appear in Chapter 12.

With whom, where, and when should you network? The short answer is: everyone, everywhere, and all the time. Given that such a universal approach is not always practical, the next chapters suggest ways to fine-tune your networking efforts.

Chapter Four

WHO SHOULD BE PART OF YOUR NETWORK?

WHAT KINDS OF CONTACTS FORM THE MOST EFFECTIVE NETWORK?

It has been said that your potential network consists of all the people you already know and everyone you've yet to meet. The people who can best contribute to your network of contacts fall into several categories. These are people who can

- Give you advice, information, or referrals to additional contacts
- Tell you about specific job openings in their own companies or other organizations they may know about
- Introduce you to people with hiring power
- Hire you immediately
- Hire you sometime in the future.

Try to build a network that is as diverse as possible and that includes at least a few highly influential people. Don't rule anyone out or assume that a particular individual can't help you.

Networking has a lot to do with looking for commonalities. Mutual

FOOT NOTE

Consultant George Moskoff advises giving serious thought to any network you attempt to construct. You will add value to your network if you consider what your contacts have in common with each other and with you. Think about reasons they might be motivated to help you and how you might be able to help them.

interests provide openings for building relationships with people in your network. And, more often than not, members of your network share something in common with you.

How you connect with such people will vary according to your tastes and preferences. You might prefer unstructured situations that enable you to seek people out one on one. In addition to identifying individuals and asking them to be part of your network, you may find that organized group membership enables you to append large networks to your own in one fell swoop (well, it might take a few swoops). Some categories of ready-made networks include

- **Groups whose members share your career or the career you aspire to.** Professional associations and organizations are the best examples of such groups, and their members are often highly effective network contacts.

- **Mixed-career groups.** Members of these groups come from all walks of life, yet a common thread has brought them together. Your local Chamber of Commerce or church group are examples. Even the people at your current place of employment can be part of this kind of group. In all likelihood, not everyone you work with shares your career, but the workplace can take on family-like qualities that lend themselves to employees helping each other. Mixed-career groups are beneficial because of the diversity of people and opportunities they expose you to.

- **Same-sex groups.** For both men and women, these types of groups spring up informally all the time. Maybe you go out with the guys to play golf or smoke cigars. It's not like when you were kids and had a treehouse with a "No girls allowed" sign, but it's unofficially understood that the group is just for the guys. Same thing on the women's side: many informal women's groups centering around children's activities. At the same time, because of women's quest for greater empowerment over the past several decades, a number of formal groups for women have sprung up, such as Business and Professional Women USA and the National Association for Female Executives. See the Resources section (Part 5) for an expanded list of networking groups for women.

THE VERY BEST KINDS OF CONTACTS FOR NEW GRADUATES

For the new college graduate, just about anyone associated with your college experience can form the foundation of a solid network. The cream of the crop includes

- **Your classmates.** They may seem like the competition, but no one knows you better. And since you will be going through the job search at roughly the same time, your college pals know what openings are out there. You will all encounter lots of information that you can share with each other.

- **Alumni, especially recent grads.** Recent alumni who've paved the way for you are intimately acquainted with the kinds of jobs you hope to land. Older, more established alumni may be far removed from the kind of entry-level job you'd like, but that also means they may have hiring power.

- **Parents.** Your parents can be rich sources of referrals for you.

- **Parents of classmates.** You knew there must have been a reason you were so polite when you visited your roommate's family back during sophomore year. Like your own parents, your friends' folks can provide a treasure trove of networking help.

- **Other relatives.** Don't be afraid to tap into the potentially rich network offered by the branches of your family tree.

- **Professors, especially your adviser.** Professors can be wonderful allies in the networking game. Teachers in your major field of study can be well connected with your career field and are certainly invested in your success.

- **Fraternity brothers, sorority sisters, and Greek organization alumni.** You've undoubtedly heard it said that you make lifelong friends in your Greek organization. That network can start working for you right away, not only with your contemporaries but with fraternity and sorority alumni, who may be able to assist you.

Networking

- **Administrators.** They may not have been your favorite people while you were in school, but those deans and vice presidents have well-established ties with some of the most prominent people in the community and beyond. Networking efforts with administrative honchos can easily pay off.

- **Coaches.** Athletic coaches can be excellent network contacts. They care about their athletes and know lots of people.

- **Guest speakers.** The professionals who come to speak to your classes are a vast untapped resource. One of my students who was interested in a career in pharmaceutical sales approached a guest speaker from that industry after the presentation and introduced herself. She asked the pharmaceutical rep if she could send him her resume. He agreed, and she kept in touch with him throughout the last semester before she graduated. By the time she claimed her diploma, she had lined up a $40,000-a-year job with the drug firm.

- **Current and former employers.** It seems as though fewer and fewer college students get through all four years without having a job at some point, whether during the summer or while in school. Even if the jobs you hold while in college are not in your career field, your employers can still be useful networking contacts.

- **Members of your religious community.** Whether your campus ministry or your congregation back home, your house of worship is a fine source of contacts. See Chapter 5 for more.

- **Members of professional organizations.** Most colleges sponsor student chapters of professional organizations, which are rich sources of networking contacts. If your college does not have such student chapters—and even if it does—your networking efforts will benefit from a student membership in the nearest professional chapter. See also Chapter 5.

- **Fellow volunteers.** Volunteer work provides abundant networking opportunities at any stage of your life, and college is a wonderful time to get started, not only in making a contribution to society, but in making some productive connections.

- **Chamber of commerce members.** If you attend meetings of the chamber of commerce in the community you wish to work in after graduation, you can make many important contacts. Consider joining the junior chamber of commerce, also known as the Jaycees, an organization especially aimed at young people aged twenty-one to thirty-nine. The National Junior Chamber of Commerce Web site (*http://www.usjaycees.org/*) describes the Jaycees as "the organization of choice for men and women twenty-one to thirty-nine years of age who want the best opportunities for leadership development, volunteerism, and community service."

- **Informational interviewees.** Informational interviewing is a goldmine of networking contacts for college students. See Part 3.

THE VERY BEST KINDS OF CONTACTS FOR ESTABLISHED JOB SEEKERS AND JOB CHANGERS

- **Members of professional organizations.** These colleagues will be among your most effective contacts. See Chapter 5 for more.

- **Your past or present co-workers.** Not every workplace has the camaraderie depicted on such classic sitcoms as *The Mary Tyler Moore Show*, but most workplaces do develop family-like qualities. Your current and former co-workers likely care a lot about you and would be eager to help you make your next career move. Don't rule out people in cities where you used to work or locales in which you'd never consider working. Even if they're far away, they may know someone in the city where you do want to work.

- **Family.** Sometimes your family is networking for you without any prompting from you, as career counselor Allison Corkey discovered. "My mother called a total stranger who worked in a position that she thought that I would be good at and should aspire to," Corkey recalls. "After a thirty-minute conversation with this person, she found out that the stranger had a part-time job coming open in a few months. My mother gave me the person's number, and I called every few days until I got an interview, and I subsequently got the job."

• **Friends you're in touch with regularly.** Of course, it almost goes without saying that your friends will be important parts of your network. Don't be afraid to call upon them.

• **Old friends, such as college buddies whom you see infrequently.** You might feel uncomfortable about seeking out people you feel you've neglected for a long time, especially when you're approaching them in a state of need. But don't forget that they may feel just as out of touch and may be eager to reestablish your friendship. And remember that since networking is a sharing process, you may be able to give them as much as they give you.

• **Members of your religious community.** Fellowship and networking are closely related. See more information in Chapter 5.

• **Fellow volunteers.** The people you meet when you're contributing to society are among the best network contacts. See Chapter 5 for more.

• **Informational interviewees.** Informational interviewing is particularly helpful for those thinking of changing jobs or careers, but the process can yield results for virtually any job seeker. See Part 3.

• **Neighbors.** Especially in close-knit neighborhoods where block parties and barbecues are common, neighbors can be matchless networking allies.

FOOT NOTE

Many colleges and universities are establishing on-line communities that are tailor-made for networking. To see if your school is listed, check out AlumniConnections.com at *http://www.alumniconnections.com.*

- **Your kids' friends' parents.** If you have kids, you undoubtedly frequently rub elbows with their friends' parents, who are fair game as part of your network.

- **Your mentor(s).** Having a mentor within your inner circle of contacts is one of the best things you can do for your career. See more about mentors in Chapter 13.

- **The people you "play" with.** Whether it's golf, softball, bridge, or jogging, the games people play make for ties that bind. See Chapter 5 for more.

- **Business associates, such as customers, clients, vendors, and suppliers.** The people on the fringes of your immediate employment sphere, but with whom you have regular dealings, are an often-overlooked source of networking contacts. Yet these may be the people who know the most about the comings and goings—and consequent vacancies—in your field.

- **People you admire in your field.** Though it may be tricky to make contact with some of these folks, people you've read articles about, you've heard speak, or who have written interesting articles themselves are wonderful additions to your network.

- **Real estate agents, financial advisers, and others.** These professionals are interested in helping you, in part because they want to keep you as a happy customer. Their business may bring them into contact with a variety of people in different fields, and they can be a useful source of contact.

FOOT NOTE

In his comprehensive networking Web site, Guy Felton offers a rich list of ideas for networking contacts. He suggests writing each classification of person on an index card and then listing people you know (or would like to know) who fall under these classifications. See his list at *http://www.careermag.com/newsarts/networking/1093.html.*

HOW MANY CONTACTS DO YOU NEED?

The consensus among networking experts is that 250 contacts is a good goal to shoot for. Why 250? Because, supposedly, everyone knows 250 people. If you were going to, say, plan your wedding, the guest list for your side of the aisle could have 250 people on it, according to Brian Krueger in his book *College Grad Job Hunter*. Does that mean you should feel inadequate if your network comes nowhere near that number? Of course not. Only a small percentage of those surveyed for this book had a network that large. Of survey respondents for this book, only 25 percent had networks of 100 people or more (and of those, only 7 percent reached the magic 250 contacts).

While it's true that the more people you network with, the more likely you may be to reach your career goals, it's equally true that the quality of the relationships you build is just as important, if not more so, than the size of your network. If your core network consists of only, say, twenty-five people, but they are people well invested in you and your success, your network is probably as big as it needs to be. To start, just sit down and brainstorm a list of everyone you know who might be a helpful network contact. Open your mind to as many people as possible. Don't rule anyone out at this point. Later, you can go back if necessary and cross off people who might be too far-fetched. In my classes, I give my students three minutes to come up with as many prospective contacts as possible. Most come up with twenty-five, thirty, or more.

Your total number of networking contacts also may be less important than setting some goals, such as gaining one contact a day, three per week, or ten each month. Or set a goal to establish a certain number of contacts at each networking-oriented event you attend. That advice paid off for a student counseled by Patrick Farrell when he was director of career services at a small, private college. The student was planning to attend a professional association recruitment program event. "I told her to set a goal to contact five people, if only to get their names and shake hands," Farrell relates. "Her third contact turned into a legitimate job offer. Had she not set the goal, she said she would have stood in the corner and watched all evening. But since she had set the goal, she felt compelled to get five names because she knew I would ask next time I saw her. Use whatever motivation works for you, but set a goal."

Chapter Five

WHERE TO NETWORK—THE TOP 50 NETWORKING HOT SPOTS

Many events and organizations (some of which are listed in the Resources section of this book) are created specifically for networking. These organizations provide copious networking opportunities, but they tend to create only short-term contacts. Because people utilize these networking groups and events primarily when they are urgently seeking a job or business contacts, long-term networking relationships are unlikely to result. Thus, the best and most meaningful networking often takes place in venues that are earmarked for other purposes.

"I network everywhere I go," says corporate training and recruiting specialist Sheila Howe. "I read the paper to find social (networking) opportunities and try not to be home unless I am making phone calls, prospecting on the Internet, organizing, or writing follow-up communications. Wherever I go, I have plenty of my personal business cards with me."

Just about anywhere that people gather is fair game for networking, but here are the top thirty that successful networkers have found especially effective, followed by twenty additional promising venues:

1. **Professional organizations.** Cited as by far the most effective networking venue by those responding to a survey for this book, professional organizations provide truly superb networking settings. As career counselor John Clark points out, "Members of professional organizations are by definition in touch with their professions and tend to be aware of upcoming openings first. Developing relationships within this framework is more than worth the effort."

   "Cultivating professional relationships with colleagues in my industry has afforded me invaluable opportunities to collect new ideas and business cards, and hear about career opportunities," points out Ohio State University career counselor B. J. O'Bruba. "The informal setting of conferences breeds a friendly and pro-networking environment." Echoes Vic Snyder, a career counselor at the University of Washington, "Having been in leadership positions in two different professional associations, I have consistently heard of job openings. [Professional association membership] has also helped me with social connections, since I am not overly extroverted. [Membership] gave me opportunities to be visible and to demonstrate abilities and strengths in a context that was relevant to most of the professionals in my field."

To maximize professional associations and organizations as a networking opportunity, be more than just a member. Volunteer to edit the organization's newsletter or coordinate the next big event. Pitch in with committee work. Offer to be program chair. Your active participation will produce indelible bonds with other members and will also allow them to see what you can do. "The best results are obtained if I become an active part of the association—take a board position, volunteer to host a committee, etc.," reports consultant Lisa LeVerrier. Vic Snyder relates that he met his current boss when he served on a professional organization committee addressing issues regarding the future of work. "I learned about her work philosophy and she mine," he recounts. "So far it is the best match I've had in a work setting."

Professional organizations often hold events specifically designed for networking, as Christine Cangiano found out. Cangiano, now director of a college career center, recalls that her first job out of college resulted from attending a professional association's networking night. "Because I did not have enough time to talk to everyone, I took down the names and numbers of the others and called them after the event," Cangiano relates. "One of the individuals thought that [my networking efforts] took so much initiative that she offered me a part-time job. I took it, and a month later, they hired me full time."

2. **Volunteer organizations.** While there certainly are good reasons to donate your time to a good cause, the side benefit of making great contacts cannot be overlooked. In fact, among respondents surveyed for this

book, volunteer work ranked as the second most effective networking venue. Some of the best-connected professionals, in fact, place volunteer work high on their agendas, according to Dawn Baskerville, writing in *Black Enterprise* magazine. Robin Fleischer, assistant director of the Career Development Center at Transylvania University, observes, "Volunteer community activity has allowed me to network with a more diverse population within various work environments, as opposed to professional networking organizations." Volunteer work tends to be one of the more visible ways to network because it gives you an opportunity to develop and demonstrate skills—not to mention the fact that people admire your selflessness and altruism. "I have been most effective when networking in volunteer organizations," notes career consultant Cynthia Fulford. "This is where I am doing what I love, and others get to see it."

Volunteers are remembered and appreciated by people in high places whom they might not otherwise meet. Baskerville cites Stanley Nelson of Norwalk, Connecticut, who says, "My municipal networking has allowed me closer access to a number of real power brokers."

Volunteer work can be especially valuable for college students because of the increasing importance of obtaining experience while still in school. The experience you list on your resume does not have to be paid experience. You can learn enormous amounts and apply transferable skills through volunteer work—networking all the while.

So go out there and help build a house through Habitat for Humanity. Become a literacy tutor. Produce a newsletter for a local charity. Volunteer your time to a community redevelopment agency. There are thousands of possibilities that will enable you to make a worthwhile contribution to society while affording you an excellent networking venue.

3. **Charity and fundraising events.** Another way to network while contributing charitably is to attend fundraising events—luncheons, dinners, fashion shows, auctions, banquets, and balls. Although they do cost more than volunteering, these events provide yet another opportunity to add helpful contacts to your network. Writing in *Black Enterprise*, Marjorie Whigham-Desir notes that attending such events can be a huge boon to those relocating to a new area. These functions can put you on the fast

track to meeting important people in a new city. Whigham-Desir advises finding out more about the cause the event supports, as well as who the sponsoring companies are. Such research will enable you to start and maintain conversations intelligently.

4. **Civic and community groups.** Your local civic association, Lions Club, Rotary Club, Kiwanis Club, Masons, Elks, Moose Lodge, and Shriners are just a few of the community groups where networking is possible.

5. **Religious community.** Both clergy and congregation members can be part of your network. "My pastor referred me to another pastor whose church was looking for a person to start a youth group for preteen children," reports DeLynn Davenport, a recruiter for an engineering placement firm. Similarly, corporate training and recruiting specialist Sheila Howe recalls how the pastor at a new church she was joining facilitated her networking efforts. "He introduced me to the congregation and let them know my profession and job-seeking status right there in front [of the church]! I was somewhat embarrassed to be put on the spot, but some members have reached out to assist me."

6. **Golf course.** Playing golf has been called the ultimate business relationship builder, an integral part of the business culture. Golf course behavior

FOOT NOTE

Dan Weilbaker, a professor at Northern Illinois University, teaches "Business Golf 101," in which, the Associated Press reports, he offers such advice as
- Use the first six holes to get to know the golfers with whom you're trying to network, the next six holes to learn more about their companies, and the last six to share ideas on how you might be able to fulfill their needs.
- Don't play poorly on purpose to let your networking partners win.
- Conversely, if you really are a mediocre golfer, pick up the ball after eight shots on each hole so as not to slow down play.

is often seen as a microcosm of the way business is conducted. "There's no doubt that the golf course continues to be a prime playground for the power game in business," writes journalist Anu Manchikanti in the *Minneapolis Star Tribune*. It's a way to cement your contacts in a relaxed atmosphere, away from the pressure cooker of the workplace—or even the power lunch. The game also can serve as a conversation starter off the course. Those who tout the golf course as the perfect venue for networking suggest that you will be left behind if you don't play golf. Golf can be a particularly important tool for networking within the company you already work for, especially if golf is deeply ingrained in the corporate culture. For neophytes, experts suggest lessons and practice so the game will go smoothly and not distract from networking.

7. **Tennis/squash/racquetball/basketball court.** For those who like to make connections while at play but don't favor golf, these court sports are often prime venues for networking.

8. **Health club/spa/YMCA.** There's something about the common goal of fitness that brings people together. Career counselor Diane Kohler describes an "embarrassing moment" in which she spotted an important networking contact at the gym. She had to decide "whether to hide or come out and face the music while hot and sweaty in gym attire." Despite being mortified, Kohler came out to meet the networking opportunity head on, and it paid off—the contact eventually hired her!

9. **Political campaigns.** The bonds you make with others while working to support a candidate you mutually believe in are among the strongest. Campaigns always welcome volunteers, and they offer marvelous opportunities to mingle with potential network contacts.

10. **Chamber of commerce.** Attending chamber meetings and events is one of the best ways to get to know the movers and shakers in your community. Chambers also frequently sponsor leadership classes that are superb not only for networking, but also for professional development.

11. **Your hometown.** Just click your heels together three times. . . . A research study by OI Partners showed that 80 percent of those polled found jobs in their hometowns, so, if you're living where you grew up, networking in your stomping grounds makes good sense. Look for the events that make your town your town. I grew up in Moorestown, New Jersey, where the big events were the PTA Fair and the Moorestown Horse Show. Everyone went. Those are the kinds of events at which I'd network if I still lived there.

12. **Airplanes.** "I travel the same route every week and share this experience with several other people," notes management consultant Christopher Maffett. "Once I start to recognize individuals, it makes it much easier to strike up a conversation about work and potential opportunities." Career consultant Terry Gillis cautions against overlooking airplane seatmates who might not seem like obvious network contacts. "I always seem to get seated next to little old ladies on planes and have often dismissed the idea that they could be helpful," Gillis notes. "One time, an older lady asked what I did. I told her I was a career consultant. It turned out that her son was in the business as well, and she provided me with his name and told me to contact him. I did, and we developed a connection over time."

13. **The favorite watering holes for your dream company/industry.** If there's a company you're just dying to work for, it makes sense to hang out where the company's denizens hang—their favorite bars, lunch spots, restaurants. You can soak up tons of company culture while connecting with key people who work there.

14. **Toastmasters.** This international organization serves as far more than a venue for networking. The group helps people overcome the fear of

 FOOT NOTE

Check to see if your own company offers a Toastmasters chapter. Many organizations do so to help employees improve communications skills.

public speaking and learn skills to enhance success. It's especially good for those who are very shy about networking. Members of Toastmasters receive constructive evaluation. It's an effective way to build confidence while building your network. Toastmaster chapters are located all over the world (check your local newspaper or phone book for one near you), but if you can't find a local branch, the Toastmasters International Web page (*http://www.toastmasters.org/*) tells you how to start one.

15. **Weddings.** There's nothing like a little networking when you're seated at a table full of strangers. One of those strangers could easily become a key part of your network.

16. **Cocktail parties.** These gatherings aren't always the best for networking since they're primarily social events—and you do have to be wary of the booze factor—but sometimes small, festive events such as cocktail parties can present lively networking opportunities, especially when they are part of business functions. You can maximize the opportunity by learning in advance who will be on the guest list and strategizing about whom you want to get to know better.

17. **Cruises.** Some organizations offer "schmooze cruises" especially designed for networking, but even your basic vacation cruise can provide opportunities to mingle.

18. **Conventions and trade shows.** The business section in the newspaper for your closest metropolitan area should contain listings of these events

FOOT NOTE

One of the most awkward aspects of networking at social events where food is served is trying to shake hands, exchange business cards, and talk while holding food and eating. Solution? If your main objective is to network at these events, eat before you go.

and tell you whether they're open to the public. Look also in trade publications for your field for event listings.

19. **Book clubs.** Spurred on by Oprah Winfrey's TV book club, community book clubs have sprung up all over the country. The stimulating intellectual atmosphere they provide lends itself well to networking.

20. **Continuing education programs.** Rapid changes in the workplace mean that continuing education and even advanced degrees are desirable for many professionals; for others, further training is an absolute requirement. In the accounting field, for example, you cannot keep your certification unless you continually brush up your skills and stay on top of new tax laws and accounting practices. But even in fields where such updating is not required, lifelong learning is beneficial because it keeps you sharp and keeps you networking. You have the added advantage of networking with those who know your field the best—the people already in it. Career counselor Lori Willeford cites graduate classes as highly effective networking venues. "Not only are these individuals classmates; they are successful professionals and more importantly, good friends," Willeford notes. "I can share my struggles, and they provide a different perspective." Faculty members and advisers are also excellent network contacts. Check with professional associations, community colleges, and universities for courses, graduate programs, workshops, seminars, and conferences that can help you refresh your skills and knowledge.

 FOOT NOTE

For listings of existing book clubs, tips on starting a book club, and news about what books other clubs are reading, check out these Web sites:
- **The Bookmarc:** *http://www.bookmarc.com/*
- **Black Book Network Book Club News:**
  http://www.blackbooknetwork.com/bookclubnews.htm
- **Go On Girl Book Club, Inc., described as the largest national reading club for black women:** *http://www.Goongirl.org/*

21. **College conferences.** If you're looking for prime networking situations, be sure you keep up to date with what's happening on local college campuses. Colleges and universities continually sponsor and/or host conferences that are superb places for networking. While some conferences are open only to members of the sponsoring organizations or college constituencies, many are open to the public. Numerous conferences include a recruiting or job-fair component. They also enable you to expand your educational horizons and enhance your professional development. To keep abreast of conferences you might attend, watch for notices in the local newspaper, subscribe to the campus newspaper, check out the school's Web page, or ask to be placed on the events-calendar mailing list.

22. **Alumni clubs, associations, reunions, and networks.** Whether you're a new graduate or have been out of school for a few years, it's hard to beat the networking potential of alumni clubs and associations. People's natural inclination is to do business with people with whom they have common bonds. Even small colleges have alumni chapters across the country that hold regular social events, which are wonderful for networking. If you can't find alumni groups in your area, make it a point to return to your alma mater for reunions whenever possible. To network with folks who are even more loyal than ordinary alumni in looking out for your interests, look to your fraternity or sorority. "When I move to a new city, the first thing I do is contact my national sorority's headquarters for information on the local alumnae chapter," reports Lara Cegala, coordinator of cooperative education at the University of Central Florida. "If there is not one, I then take the initiative to organize

FOOT NOTE

Don't forget that alumni magazines and other publications can be rich sources of networking contacts. You can discover long-lost classmates who might be helpful, as well as identify alumni you don't know but with whom you have something in common.

and form a new chapter. I have found that this is an effective way for me to meet new people and network with women in the community. People think that sorority membership is just for collegiate women, when really alumnae benefit from membership one hundred times more. I have met some terrific women and have made many connections that have helped me personally and professionally."

23. **Ex-employer alumni clubs.** Just as college alumni clubs are valuable for networking because of the common bonds and memories you share with fellow members, ex-employer alumni clubs can offer the same benefits. A number of large corporations have formed alumni clubs, such as the Time-Life Alumni Society and Xerox-X. Who better than people in your own current or former industry to include in your network? They know where you've been and where you could be going.

24. **Tea parties.** On the heels of fascination with wines and coffees comes this new trend, particularly popular with women. Tearoom-type restaurants, where customers go to feel pampered while they enjoy their tea and scones, have sprung up in many cities, and the relaxed settings are perfect for networking with other professionals.

25. **Theme parks.** What's the one thing you're likely to spend the majority of your time doing at a theme park? Waiting in line. Make the most of those long waits by striking up conversations with other members of the queue.

26. **Newspaper business section.** Almost every newspaper dedicates a portion of its business section to the professional comings and goings of people in the paper's readership area. These sections feature blurbs, often accompanied by photos, about people who have been hired or promoted by local companies and organizations. If you scan these sections regularly, you are bound to find someone you either know or have something in common with. I had lost touch with a dear friend who was matron of honor at my wedding, for example, but one day I spotted her smiling face in a photo in my local paper's business section—she had

just been hired to a new position. The news gave me a perfect entree to reconnect with her. The same process can work for anyone. If you see an item about someone you've lost touch with, you have an excellent opportunity to call or write and say, "Congratulations on the promotion! Let's get together for lunch soon." It's also possible to network with strangers through these newspaper sections, although you need a little more boldness than you do when you contact people from your past. But let's say you see an item about someone who went to your college and is now working at a company you'd love to work for. It certainly would not be unreasonable to contact the person and say, "I'm a fellow graduate of Cornell, and I saw the item in the paper about your new job with Zapware. Congratulations! I wondered if you'd be interested in having lunch sometime to compare notes about Cornell and our careers."

Business sections also provide helpful networking information outside of these "comings and goings" columns. Any news of change—new markets, expansions, mergers, and acquisitions, as well as new products or services, can signal that a company will have openings and that people in that company will be worthwhile targets of your networking. "Focus on anything change-related, because change means opportunity," writes William S. Frank on his CareerLab Web site.

The Internet affords networkers the opportunity to make some powerful connections with folks they might never meet in person but who can be extremely helpful in career development. A number of on-line venues are available:

27. **On-line discussion groups,** also known as special-interest groups, forums, or Listserv electronic mail lists (so called because of the Listserv software that operates them). Thousands of discussion groups on virtually every conceivable topic are available. It's not hard to find a group that centers on your professional or personal interests. For example, I belong to an on-line discussion group for career counselors called Jobplace, operated by the National Association of Colleges and Employers. It was through Jobplace that I connected with many of the

career counselors quoted in this book. In the past, I've belonged to groups for writers, public information officers, people interested in women's studies, and others. Members generally interact with these discussion groups through e-mail. To join a group, you send a subscription command to a specific address, which is handled by the operation software that manages the group. Once you are on the subscription list, every message you send to the group goes to all members. Thus, every time I send a message to Jobplace, it goes to some seventeen hundred subscribers; so I am, in a very real sense, networking with those seventeen hundred people simultaneously. Many discussion groups are now Web-based, enabling you to interact with them through your Web browser instead of by e-mail. Members of the group have the opportunity to ask questions, obtain career advice, and access the many job postings sent to the group. How to find out what groups are available and how to subscribe to them? A number of search engines, such as The Lizst, enable networkers to identify and subscribe to groups. See the Resources section for more information.

28. **Usenet groups, also known as newsgroups.** Usenet groups are similar to on-line discussion groups, but they function in a different realm of the Internet; instead of having newsgroup messages come to you via e-mail, you have to go to a particular location on the Internet to read and respond to the messages. The topics for Usenet groups cover an even broader spectrum than those for on-line discussion groups, some of them highly specialized and even some off-the-wall. Usenet group topics lean a bit more toward personal than professional interests, but they can still be incredible venues for networking. (Bonus: Many Usenet newsgroups are totally devoted to job listings.) Interaction with Usenet groups was once possible only if your Internet service provider had special newsreader software, but today, the major Web browsers, such as Netscape Communicator and Microsoft's Internet Explorer, enable you to interact with Usenet newsgroups. How to find out about and join Usenet newsgroups? As with on-line discussion groups, special search engines can track down groups in your areas of interest. One of the best known is Deja.com. (More information can

be found in the Resources section.) Once you've identified a Usenet newsgroup, send a message out as a feeler, but avoid needy-sounding subject lines such as "Seeking Job in Engineering Field." Instead, chose a provocative subject line that questions or comments on trends or topical issues in the field. That way, newsgroup members will be more likely to read and respond to your message. Stick to that subject within your posting to the group, but mention within the message that you are looking for a job. One caution: In the past few years, Usenet groups have lost some of their charm because many of them have been inundated with "spam," messages sent to multiple Usenet groups with content that doesn't relate to the topic of the group—such as pornography and get-rich-quick schemes. To avoid spam, choose your groups carefully. Some browsers and Internet service providers also offer ways to filter out spam.

29. **Chat rooms.** Available on the Web or through such providers as America Online, chat rooms also revolve around a wide variety of professional and personal interest areas. The advantage these chat areas have over on-line discussion groups or Usenet newsgroups is that they allow real-time conversation. A message sent to an e-mail address or Usenet group might sit for anywhere from a few minutes to a few days or longer without getting a response, while chat-room input generally gets an instant response. Chat rooms provide good networking opportunities because of the way they simulate actual conversation. Other variations on the chat room include AOL's Instant Messaging and ICQ ("I seek you"), another format that allows conversation in real time. See more about chat rooms in the Resources section.

30. **Web-based networks.** A number of sites available on the Web enable you to locate people with common interests who may even be able to help your career. IndustryInsite, for example, enables you to find people on-line who share common experiences with you—same career field, same high school, same college, same current or former employers, and more. Not only can you locate people with whom you can network about your career, but many members of IndustryInsite have signed up

UNUSUAL NETWORKING VENUES

Survey respondents were asked about the most unusual or creative networking venues they had employed. Here's how they answered:

- In the lobby during intermission at a theatrical performance
- At a movie theater when the movie projector broke down
- On a ski lift
- While watching a softball game
- In a cadaver lab
- During a real-estate transaction
- Walking past a county office building and stopping to chat with other passersby
- While stranded at an airport
- During a daily subway commute
- On the sidelines of children's soccer or basketball games
- During a daughter's overnight school trip
- As a car-accident witness
- At a family member's graduation
- As the keynote speaker at a senior graduation breakfast
- In the Metro in Paris
- As a volunteer newsletter writer for a place of worship
- While serving as student senate president in college
- While serving as a dental assistant during a dental procedure
- In the hospital while recovering from surgery
- While volunteering at a reunion activity
- While helping others paint a house
- At a nail salon
- While getting a haircut
- In the swimming pool of a friend's apartment
- While ordering office supplies

- At a 5K race
- While training for a marathon
- At a shopping mall
- In line at the grocery store
- While performing in a skit
- During dance lessons
- In swim aerobics class
- At a scrapbooking social
- While building a custom home
- At an outdoor concert
- Aboard a ship ("I was hosting a trade mission to Norway and had an ideal captive market because they couldn't go anywhere else!")

to be mentors and/or volunteer resume critiquers. It's a terrific free service with enormous potential. Another interesting Web site is the Company of Friends, *Fast Company* magazine's global readers' network. More than ten thousand business people, and what the magazine's editors call "thought leaders and change agents," from all over the world have signed up. Using Company of Friends, members are organizing local discussion groups, mentoring and networking organizations, and creative problem-solving teams. See more about these Web-based venues in the Resources section.

The best of the rest:

31. Homeowners' or tenants' associations
32. Travel clubs
33. Clubs centered around hobbies
34. Sports teams and leagues (softball, bowling, Ping-Pong, etc.)

35. Dog shows, horse shows, cat shows

36. Jury duty

37. Ballroom dance lessons

38. Park benches

39. Wine tastings

40. Computer-user groups

41. Art exhibition/gallery openings

42. Waiting rooms (your auto mechanic's, doctor's, dentist's, or attorney's offices)

43. Baptisms/christenings

44. Resorts

45. Museums

46. Your favorite beach, lake, or pool

47. Investment clubs

48. Coffee shops

49. Your kids' school functions

50. Family reunions

Chapter Six

WHEN TO NETWORK

For optimal career development, networking should be an ongoing process. Virtually all networking experts advise that you should not wait until you're in crisis to begin networking. When you're in serious job-hunting mode— as a new graduate seeking your first job or as a career veteran who has decided to move on—you probably won't find a scattershot approach effective. Instead, you will likely find it beneficial to set up a networking timetable to help you set goals. Two such suggested timetables follow:

NETWORKING TIMETABLE FOR NEW GRADUATES

Recommendations from college career counselors as to when college students should begin networking range from freshman year to the middle or end of the junior year. (Keep in mind that this suggested timetable deals primarily with networking activities related to the hidden job market; you should simultaneously pursue opportunities in the open job market, such as registering with your campus career services office, attending interviews with on-campus recruiters, and scanning want ads in publications and on the Internet.)

FRESHMAN YEAR

Certainly freshman year is not too early to get to know your professors, especially your adviser. Getting to know your fellow students, a process that happens naturally in the collegiate experience, will also lay the networking groundwork in your first year of college. A good way to meet as many other students as possible is to become involved in as many organizations and activities as your academic schedule will permit you to handle. Be a curious friend; finding out as much as possible about your classmates and their interests, and about their families' and parents' occupations, can provide valuable information that you may want to recall as you get closer to graduation. Be sure to reciprocate with information that will help others. Freshman year is also the time to consider whether you might want to join a fraternity or sorority. And, if you are holding down a job to help with college expenses, establish relationships with your boss and co-workers.

SOPHOMORE YEAR

By sophomore year, you are probably beginning to narrow down your career goals, which makes this an excellent time to embark on a series of informational interviews that will help bring your career into focus. (Informational interviews are explained in depth in Part 3.) You should be continuing to forge ties with professors, other students, and people you work with. You may be starting to think about obtaining an internship in your career field for the summer between your sophomore and junior years or for part of your junior year in school. That internship can yield excellent network contacts since it's presumably in your career field. If your career goal is well defined at this point, sophomore year is a good time to join a student chapter of a professional organization (or obtain a student membership to a regular chapter).

JUNIOR YEAR

Junior year is key. Start your most serious networking push now by doing the following:

- Develop your resume, if you have not done so already. You should have your resume ready so that you can ask some of your network contacts to critique it. You also want to have it ready in case someone you meet asks for it. You may not be in a position to accept a job at this point, but you could gain an internship opportunity by having your resume ready. And any employer who takes your resume now, when you're not ready to accept a job, can be approached again closer to graduation. Start carrying copies of your resume wherever you go in case an opportunity presents itself.

- Begin to brainstorm a list of potential networking contacts (see Chapter 4). See if you can approach that magic number of 250, but don't beat yourself up if you can't. Any number is a good start, and the list is sure to grow.

- Also, make a list of companies you'd like to work for and start thinking about who you know who might be able to help you break into your dream companies.

- Sign up with one or more networking sites on the World Wide Web, such as IndustryInsite or Company of Friends. Search for and contact people in your prospective career field and preferred geographic area. Find out if your campus career services office keeps a database of alumni who could be added to your network. Check the alumni files of your fraternity or sorority, too.

- Join one or more on-line discussion groups or Usenet newsgroups in your area of professional interest. Ask the members' advice on breaking into your field.

- Step up the pace of informational interviews. You may want to set an informational interview goal; one interview a month is probably achievable while you're in school. People working in your dream companies are excellent targets for these interviews.

- Consider creating a "networking card," a business card for those not yet employed (see Chapter 11), so you have something tangible to hand out to people you meet.

- Begin to introduce yourself to every guest speaker in your field of interest who visits your classes or organization meetings. Introduce yourself to speakers in other fields who could serve as good network contacts. Give them your networking card, and if appropriate, your resume.

- Continue schmoozing with professors, students, and employers.

- Become increasingly active in professional organizations.

- If you have not yet done an internship or otherwise obtained practical experience in your career field, set the wheels in motion to do so before the middle of your senior year, and establish contact with as many people as possible at your internship workplace.

SENIOR YEAR

Networking activities should be a major focus of your senior year.

- Decide where you want to live after graduation. Most soon-to-be graduates either decide to go wherever their first job takes them, or else they decide where they want to be and pursue jobs in that region. If you are in the latter category, the beginning of your senior year is the time to decide where you want to be.

- If necessary, narrow down your list of dream employers based on geography, and strategize ways to contact key people in your dream companies.

- Join professional and mixed-industry organizations in your targeted geographic area (or transfer your student membership to the professional chapters). If it's not practical for you to attend meetings of these organizations, ask the membership chair for a membership list so that you can start making contact with members.

- Meet with your adviser early in your senior year for an in-depth discussion of your career goals, and ask for her suggestions for people you should contact.

- Continue to maintain contact with professors, students, employers, guest speakers, and folks you've "met" through on-line networking efforts.

- Find out if your university or academic department has any kind of formal mentoring program and ask to be matched with a mentor. If no program exists, try to scout out a mentor on your own. Alumni often make especially good mentors.

- Fine-tune your list of potential network contacts and set a goal to contact a certain number of these each week or month. For the first half of your senior year, connecting with a few contacts each week should be sufficient. As the countdown to graduation begins in your final semester, you may want to try for at least one a day. Arrange to meet with as many contacts as possible, and always ask each one for more referrals. Send thank-you notes, and update your contacts regularly on your progress.

- Continue informational interviewing.

- Begin to contact people with whom you conducted informational interviews earlier in your college career to tell them that you are getting close to graduation and remain very interested in their organizations (See Part 4).

- Enjoy your graduation ceremony with a big smile on your face, because if you've done all of the above, you are probably graduating with a job in hand. Be sure to write one more note to all your contacts telling them about your new job. And don't throw away any of your networking information; sometimes that first job doesn't work out, and you just might need to call upon your network again.

NETWORKING TIMETABLE FOR ESTABLISHED JOB SEEKERS AND JOB CHANGERS

For those who are already established in a career and are looking for a new job, the pace of networking varies considerably depending on whether you find yourself suddenly and unexpectedly unemployed, or whether you're comfortably employed but have decided it's time to switch jobs or careers.

Let's first establish a couple of premises:

The savviest careerists maintain their networks at all times, even while happily employed. That way they don't have to scramble to build a network if they suddenly find themselves out of work.

The better developed your network is when you begin to seek a new job, the shorter your job search is likely to be.

Now, let's assume a fast-track pace for the unexpectedly unemployed; those who have the leisure of taking their time to find a new job or career can adapt this timetable to a less urgent clip. And let's assume the worst-case scenario—that the suddenly out-of-work job seeker does not have a well-established network.

• Brainstorm a list of potential contacts. Try to think of as many as you can.

• Realize that looking for a job should be almost a full-time job in itself. Plan to devote a significant portion of every day both to traditional open-market job-hunting activities (such as scanning and responding to want ads) and to networking.

• Set a goal to connect with a certain number of contacts a day. The number will depend on the urgency of your job search and your financial situation. If it's very urgent, a goal of twenty contacts a day would not be unreasonable; if it's less urgent, five a day may fill the bill.

The career fair, frequently targeted at college students but sometimes at other experienced workers, is an interesting hybrid of traditional job-search methods and networking. Sometimes interviews conducted at these fairs or expos are planned and highly structured, but the career fair format also allows for considerable informal interviewing, where networking skills are paramount. If you attend a career fair, be prepared to answer such typical questions as "Tell me about yourself," and "Why do you want to work for _____ company or in the _____ industry?" A room filled with dozens of recruiters gives you the opportunity to build rapport and relationships with those in the most desirable companies. For more about how to make the most of a career fair, visit Randall Hansen's Web article, "The Ten Keys to Success at Job and Career Fairs," at *http://www.quintcareers.com/job_career_fairs.html* or the on-line chapter of Brian Krueger's *College Grad Job Hunter*, entitled "Job Fair Success," at *http://www.collegegrad.com/ezine/15jobfair.shtml*.

- Realize that even though there may be people on your list you'd be more comfortable writing to before you phone them, you may not have that luxury. The telephone may need to be your main networking tool when you're on a fast track; e-mail is an option as well.

- Begin establishing contacts, keeping in mind the goals of seeking advice, more referrals, and face-to-face meetings. Some of those meetings may be informational interviews, depending on your situation. Be sure to send thank-you notes to everyone who is even remotely helpful.

- Be on the lookout for events you can attend and organizations you can join to enhance your networking efforts, but don't make these your major focus (unless you are comfortably employed, in which case you can allow organization- and event-oriented networking to take priority over your daily routine of establishing new contacts). Squeeze in meetings and events whenever you can, and always try to give out business cards and resumes.

- At the end of your first two to three weeks of networking, go back and reconnect with your initial list of contacts. Tell them how you're doing, and ask for any new ideas or referrals.

- If you are still unemployed at the end of the first month, begin the cycle again. Expand your list of contacts, based in part on new referrals your initial contacts have given you.

FOOT NOTE

Kate Wendleton, founder of the Five O'Clock Club, expands on the common wisdom that job hunting is a full-time job and that networking full time is extremely difficult when you're already employed. She suggests taking vacation days one day at a time, say every other Friday, and use those days for networking and interviews.

LIFELONG NETWORKING

If you haven't already picked up on the hint that networking over the long haul of your career is the best approach, let's make that clear right here. Ideally, networking that begins sometime while you're in college and continues almost until retirement time enables you to build a network of contacts, associates, and productive relationships. If networking is an ongoing process, you have a solid support system to fall back on when you need to find a job. You also have copious sources for perspectives and advice that will aid your career development, along with people to talk to and receive support from when you have troubles on the job. After all, the average worker today is expected to change careers some five times over the course of his working life, so a well-developed network can only make all the transitions easier.

So, in addition to all your regularly scheduled activities that present both organized and spontaneous networking opportunities, you might also want to set aside a certain chunk of time every week—a couple of hours perhaps—for individual networking. Write letters, make phone calls, send e-mails just to touch base with members of your network.

FOOT NOTE

The National Association of Female Executives advises going through your Rolodex or other networking database every six months to see which people you haven't talked to recently. Regularly reconnect with your most valuable players.

PART·TWO

THE NITTY-GRITTY OF

NETWORKING

Chapter Seven

THE PSYCHOLOGY OF ASKING FOR ASSISTANCE

For many people, the most daunting aspect of networking is getting past the idea of asking for help. We don't want to seem as though we're begging or groveling or worse—using people. But the fact is that most people like to be asked for assistance. Being asked for advice flatters people and makes them feel important. Knowing that someone values their expertise inspires most people to go out of their way to help. People feel like heroes when they can help you achieve your career ambitions. Asking and helping create a bond between you and your network contact.

Benjamin Franklin said, "If you want to make a friend, let someone do you a favor." (I blatantly stole the use of that quote from Christopher Matthews, who cites Franklin in his book, *Hardball*, about how the game of politics is played.) The art of letting people do you favors, which Matthews contends is a key facet of political success, is also one of the best routes to effective networking. "Contrary to what many people assume," Matthews writes, "the most effective way to gain a person's loyalty is not to do him

 FOOT  NOTE

Don't assume that even those closest to you have an intimate grasp on exactly what kind of work you want to do and how you're qualified, advises Guy Felton in his networking Web site. You may have to spend some time with your contacts, perhaps over lunch or dinner, to give them a full understanding of what you're looking for and what you have to offer. You might feel silly handing your resume to your closest pals, but they can help you much more effectively with it than without it.

or her a favor, but to let that person do one for you." Matthews explains that when you enlist someone's aid, you are soliciting that person's investment in you and your success. The person not only feels good about helping you now, but watches out for you in the future to make sure her faith in you was not misplaced. "Those who give you one helping hand very often make a habit of looking out for you further down the road," Matthews writes. "We tend naturally to remember the people we 'discover' along the way and seek to ensure that they prove us correct."

A significant part of networking is the process of simply talking to people about their work, learning what they like and don't like about it, and determining how and where you might fit into the same kind of work. If there's one thing people like discussing, it's their work. Work, after all, is a big part of our lives. And most people just love to talk about their jobs, which is why informational interviewing (Part 3) is so effective.

People also enjoy the sense of belonging they feel when you ask them to be part of your personal network. As long as you observe the rules of networking etiquette (Chapter 10), you should not be perceived as a user.

All of this is not to say that networking should be a one-sided endeavor. You should share as much as you can with your network contacts. Do allow your contact to determine how he can best be of assistance. Just don't be afraid to ask for that advice and assistance in the first place.

The Nitty-Gritty

Chapter Eight

CONTACTS BEGET CONTACTS: GETTING YOUR NETWORK TO WORK FOR YOU

Ever heard that theory—subject of a Broadway play and a film—that between every ordinary person and a celebrity, there are only six degrees of separation? The same could be said of networking. Because your network has the potential to expand exponentially, there may be six degrees of separation—give or take a few—between you and your next employer. That was roughly the phenomenon that one financial markets economist/analyst experienced. "Just out of graduate school, I hoped to work on Wall Street and had a few interviews set up," she relates. "No one actually had a job to offer. One person told me he had hired someone else, but he gave me that person's boss's name to see if I could get their job! It was a government job, and there were hiring freezes in many departments, but that person gave me another name to call, who gave me another name to call, and eventually I ended up working in the White House, for the president's economic adviser, all from following up on these referrals."

Earlier we noted that the average person potentially has 250 people in his or her network. But here's the real kicker. If you have a possible 250 people in your network, each person in your network also has a possible 250 people in his or her network—so your network has the potential to

FOOT NOTE

Syndicated business columnist Mark McCormack recommends passing on "heads-up" information to members of your network, which might include news about the plans of a company that is your contact's competitor.

grow almost endlessly. Some people actually have networks that vast; others neither have nor need such a massive support system. What's gratifying to know is that your network always has the potential to expand, and at any given time, you could have a lot of people invested in your success and helping you achieve it.

Your network can work for you even when you're not giving it your full attention, as career counselor Vic Snyder discovered. "[I left a job in] a technical college setting twelve years ago without a definite plan of what I wanted to do next," Snyder recalls. "Within a month a colleague contacted me to do consulting work in a vocational rehabilitation setting, and that helped me decide to start my own private practice and consulting firm. My colleague knew that I was available through my network. It was working even though I didn't know it."

THE CIRCLE PARADIGM

One way to look at how your network can work for you is to think of it as a series of overlapping circles. The innermost circle consists of your closest and most trusted friends and advisers. These are the people you would turn to first in a time of crisis—say, if you lost your job. Working outward, the next circle is the people you don't know quite as well but do feel comfortable

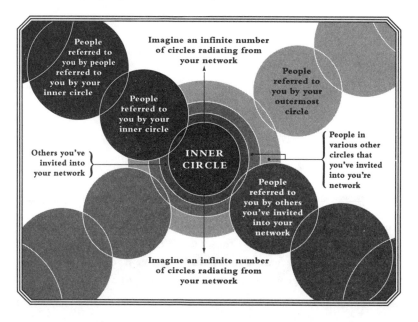

asking to be part of your network. Another circle is the people whom those in your inner circle refer you to. Another consists of the people referred by those in your outer circle. Further circles projecting outward are referrals made by your referrals. And so on. . . .

THE THEORY OF WEAK TIES

While we may think of those in the inner circle as being the most helpful members of our networks, *Money* magazine reported on a study about networking, indicating that "weak ties may have more networking potential than strong ones. Intimate ties, those of families, close friends, and business partners, the study shows, create tight circles. Since acquaintances are people who move in other groups, they usually have more range."

Of those weak ties, according to writer Donna Clark, the type that may be of the greatest help to you is someone who has been contacted by a member of your network who has paved the way for you. The contacted person is expecting to hear from you. Writing in the *Business Journal* of Charlotte, North Carolina, Clark says this "target network" should also include hiring managers in companies you'd like to work for. A particularly effective way to network with hiring managers is through informational interviews (Part 3).

FOOT NOTE

Your contacts will be much more likely to work for you if you demonstrate sincere concern for them. Writer John Garcia notes, "I see a lot of job seekers each week, but I only seem to remember those who have taken a genuine interest in me and my company."

Chapter Nine

NETWORKING FOR THE SHY AND INTIMIDATED

Think everyone who successfully networks must be a gregarious extrovert? The vast majority (70 percent) of respondents surveyed for this book described themselves not as extremely outgoing but somewhere in between gregarious and shy. Most people possess some degree of shyness and unease with the idea of networking—and some are extremely uncomfortable with the idea. But there is hope for the very shy and intimidated. Just recognizing that few people are unreserved extroverts is half the battle, as Deborah Kubena learned. "I can sometimes be quite shy when it comes to approaching people I don't know," notes Kubena, a career counselor. "When I find myself hesitating to meet people, though, I remind myself that others are probably just as uncomfortable, and that [knowledge] gives me the courage to introduce myself first. Looking back, I can't remember a time when I've regretted making the first move." In addition to realizing you're far from the only one who is shy, here are some tips for the introverted networker:

• Start your networking efforts in settings where you know other participants, such as professional organizations.

• When trying to make one-on-one connections, such as for informational interviewing purposes, start with those you've been referred to by family members and close friends and work your way up to people with whom you have a common bond, such as fellow alumni of your college or high school.

• While you should avoid using as a crutch on-line methods of networking that keep you out of the social fray, the shy person can learn to get the most out of on-line discussion groups, Usenet newsgroups, Web-based networking, and chat rooms (as described in Chapter 5).

- The pen is mightier than the phone, at least for the shy person. Writing to people you've been referred to is a superb way to introduce yourself and break the ice. Writing (or e-mailing) before phoning eases you into making network connections one on one. Writing gives you an opening for when you do call: "I'm calling to follow up on the letter I wrote you last week."

- When someone you know has referred you to someone you don't know, you can often ask your acquaintance to pave the way for you by calling and telling the stranger to expect to hear from you. That way, your phone call is made a little easier because you can say, "Hi, this is Sally Johnson. I believe Jeff Barnes told you I'd be calling."

- You are eventually going to have to pick up the phone and call people you don't know. You can write or e-mail first, but sooner or later, you'll have to call. What is the best advice on how to go about it if you're shy? Just do it. Skip Haley, a self-proclaimed introvert interviewed on the CareerLab Web site by William Frank, has this to say about picking up the phone: "I absolutely hate it. But isn't it interesting—every time you do it, something good comes of it?"

- Haley also suggests reminding yourself what will happen if you don't overcome your shyness and get out to events where networking takes place. "If you don't, you're not going to meet people. And if you don't meet people, you're not going to get a job."

FOOT NOTE

The buddy system is another effective defense against shyness at networking events. Pair up with a friend and make the rounds together.

- Plan out what you will say when you make phone contacts. You may even want to have a script in front of you, such as those in Chapter 12. Just don't ever sound as though you're reading from a script. A bare-bones outline with key words will keep you from forgetting what you want to say while ensuring that you sound natural.

- When you first attend a meeting of a professional organization, learn as much as you can about the group. Read the organization's publications. When attending events where networking is likely to take place, arrive a little early and introduce yourself to the organizer or host. You may even want to call ahead of time and explain that this is your first time and you're trying to get the lay of the land. That way, you have someone who can introduce you to others at the event. If you stand near the door, advises Leslie Smith of the National Association of Female Executives, people may assume you are one of the organizers and introduce themselves to you.

- Even if you're feeling uneasy, try to smile and project enthusiasm and confidence. Networking for the shy and introverted is something of a performance. Sometimes you have to be a good actor. Even shy individuals are capable of acting like confident people. You simply have to step into your self-assured persona. You can slip back into the shy identity you're more comfortable with after you've accomplished what you need to. Does this basically amount to faking it—pretending to be someone you're not? Probably not. You're just using the tools within you to get a job done. They may not be tools you enjoy using every day, but they are tools you can employ when you need them.

FOOT NOTE

One good strategy is to redirect your shyness toward helping others have a productive time, says the National Association for Female Executives. If you pretend it's your party and your responsibility to ensure everyone's enjoyment, you can relegate your shyness to the back burner.

- Be aware of your surroundings and adapt your approach to the setting. If you're at an event where networking is the main focus, you can adopt your go-getter persona. But if it's a social event, hang back a bit and wait for appropriate openings before you make networking contacts. Look for people who are by themselves. They are likely to be just as shy as you and would love to be approached. Making eye contact with people throughout the room and smiling will encourage them to gravitate to you. Turn the tables on your shy self by making it your mission to make others feel at home and relaxed.

- Be sure you're up on current events when you attend an affair where networking may take place. Topical issues—including sports—are always great icebreakers (as long as they're not too controversial). It also doesn't hurt to have read some of the latest books and seen current movies (or at least read the reviews). Bone up on current issues in your field as well by reading trade and professional journals. Prepare some leading questions that will break the ice and get people to talk. Be curious and interested. Ask people lots of questions about themselves and their jobs. They'll love answering you, and you'll have less talking to do. But you'll still make a good connection because you gave someone a chance to talk about himself or herself.

- Many of us are shy about networking because we fear rejection. Ask yourself: What's the worst thing that could happen? Someone you meet could be standoffish; someone you ask for advice may hesitate to give it. Whatever you do, don't take it personally. Just tell yourself it's no big deal and move on.

- If your biggest fear is not that others will react badly but that you will say or do something stupid, lighten up. Everyone, even the most polished professionals, make a silly and embarrassing mistake now and then. Learn to laugh off your gaffes.

- Set goals for yourself. Whether it's making five phone calls a day, exchanging three business cards at an event, or adding one new person a day to your network, you will be more likely to rise above your shyness if you set and meet goals. Take a break in between each step toward your goal, and reward yourself with a little treat when you meet each goal— eating a favorite food, soaking in a hot bath, renting a good movie— whatever feels like a reward to you. And don't give up when you don't meet your goals.

• Celebrate your successes. It's almost a sure bet that you'll have more successes than you expect and more successes than failures. Bask in your triumphs and let the momentum encourage you to be a little less shy the next time.

Chapter Ten

NETWORKING ETIQUETTE

"People don't mind being used," writes Christopher Matthews in *Hardball*. "what they mind is being taken for granted." Author and public speaker Jeff Roberts describes how his wife was left feeling used and betrayed by a thoughtless job seeker. "My wife, a human resources professional, was burned once by someone who used her in networking," Roberts relates. "The experience left her extremely cautious in helping others. A fellow co-worker lost her job and asked my wife if she knew anyone in field X. My wife went out of her way to set this co-worker up with a friend who was prominent in field X. Naturally the friend assisted the co-worker. However the co-worker never spoke one word in appreciation for the lead or ever talked with my wife again until she needed another lead. I urge all people using networking to remember the relationship dimensions of the experience. Make sure that you bend over backwards to let the people know of your appreciation for their assistance." Beyond the simple courtesy of showing your appreciation (see sample thank-you notes in Part 4), some other aspects of networking etiquette are worth keeping in mind:

- **Know your purpose for networking.** It sounds obvious, but some job seekers waste their contacts' time without really knowing what they want to do, where they want to work, or how the contact might be helpful to them.

- **Do your homework.** Don't ask your contacts questions that could easily have been answered by doing a little basic research. The more you know about your contacts' companies and backgrounds, the more impressed they will be with you.

- **Don't act desperate.** The smell of fear emanating from a networking job seeker can be a real turn-off. Your contacts will be much more willing to help someone who is confident and capable than someone groveling and desperate. Be positive and upbeat. Smile! "If you have fun, they'll have fun," writes William Frank in his CareerLab Web site. "If they have fun, they'll like you. If they like you, they're more likely to help you or hire you."

- **Remember that networking is a two-way street.** Offer your help to your contacts and supply needed information whenever possible. Writing in the *Arizona Business Gazette*, Mark McCormack talks about attending Jaycee events where many attendees were there solely for what they could take from the group—contacts, business cards, sales leads. But by offering to organize a golf event for the group, McCormack built a reputation as a giver instead of a taker. And when you do offer help, follow through with your promises.

- **Listen.** When a contact is kind enough to offer you advice, listen attentively. Don't monopolize the conversation. Don't rush through the conversation and start to seek out the next person before you're finished with your current conversation partner.

- **Respect your contacts' time.** Don't drop into a contact's office uninvited, and when you call a current or prospective member of your network, always ask if he or she has time to talk. Even when the answer is yes, make your conversation brief and to the point. Also, be aware of time zones if you contact people in other parts of the country. A sleepy Californian would not appreciate a call made at 9 A.M. New York time.

FOOT NOTE

A critical component of any networker's etiquette kit should be breath mints. Don't leave home without them.

- **Get permission** before using a network contact's name to approach another prospective contact. Similarly, when you're scouting for new members of your network, tell prospective contacts how you got their names.

- **Be careful as to your use of the word "networking."** While it's generally quite effective to ask people if they'd be willing to be part of your personal network, some people have grown weary of being "networked." Unless you are attending a function specifically earmarked for networking, it's best not to advertise the fact that that is what you are doing. Instead, think of yourself as making connections, building relationships, and seeking advice.

- **Don't be pushy and aggressive.** Be sensitive to just how much a contact is willing to do for you, and don't push beyond that limit.

Chapter Eleven

SELL THE SIZZLE:
ADVERTISING THE PRODUCT (YOU)

For many people, one of the more intimidating aspects of networking is the marketing and sales element. Building relationships is wonderfully rewarding, but those relationships will prove all the more fruitful to your career if you can also sell your network contacts on how wonderful you are. Most of us like to talk about ourselves—or at least we are less uncomfortable talking about ourselves than we are in talking about other topics. When you network, you always tread a fine line between the confident and the boastful—the scintillating raconteur relating fascinating tales of accomplishment and the crashing bore who alienates everyone with his bombast.

YOUR UNIQUE SELLING PROPOSITION

The first trick to selling yourself is to identify the one thing about you that makes you unique among job seekers. What's the one thing you do better than anyone else? In advertising, the one thing that makes a product better than any other is its Unique Selling Proposition. Is it easy to come up with one thing you do better than anyone else? Nope. But identifying something about yourself that makes you especially appealing to employers will help not only with your networking efforts but also with the entire marketing campaign that comprises your job search. Once you've identified your Unique Selling Proposition, you can make it the centerpiece of three types of one-on-one networking communications: the sound bite, the commercial, and the infomercial.

THE SOUND BITE

The sound bite, a concept introduced by Brian Krueger in his *College Grad Job Hunter*, is a very short introduction of yourself used in situations where you are meeting a lot of people and probably not spending a great deal of time with any one of them. Events specifically designed for networking are ideal for the sound bite, which lasts about fifteen to twenty seconds and may or may not be the prelude to a lengthier conversation. The trick is to make your sound bite so intriguing that people will want to spend more time talking with you. The sound bite also might be incorporated into an initial phone conversation with a prospective new member of your network.

At its most basic level, the sound bite's structure is this:

> Hi, my name is _____. I'm in the _____ field, and I'm looking to _____.

The last blank would be filled in with your current career aspiration, whether to stay within your field and move up, or move into a different career.

A college student or new graduate might add the following to the basic structure:

> Hi, my name is _____. I will be graduating/I just graduated from _____ with a degree in _____. I'm looking to _____.

You can stick with the sound bite's basic structure and see where it takes you, or you can add an element of intrigue by incorporating your Unique Selling Proposition. Let's look, for example, at how a conversation might go that starts with an intriguing sound bite:

> *Networker #1:* Hi, my name is Carmen Southwick. I deal in dreams.
> *Networker #2:* How do you do that?
> *Networker #1:* I'm a wedding planner. I plan dream weddings for couples. I've been working for myself, but I'd like to get in with one of the big resorts that puts on weddings.

As you can imagine, the ensuing conversation now has considerable potential. Let's look at another example:

Networker #1: Hi, my name is Ned Peters. I turn animals into smiles.

Networker #2: How so?

Networker #1: I manage a pet store and love to watch children's eyes light up when I put a little animal in their hands. I'm training to use pet therapy in hospitals and nursing homes and hope to break into that field.

And one more:

Networker #1: Hi, my name is Betty Joiner. I train future leaders.

Networker #2: This I've got to hear about.

Networker #1: I'm a teacher! I love shaping the minds of the next generation, but I'm also interested in getting into corporate training.

The concern, of course, with the intriguing sound bite is that you'll sound corny or hokey. And, in fact, chances are you will. But you will also hook your conversation partner into finding out more about you. You just have to decide whether or not you're comfortable with incorporating an intriguing line into your sound bite; if not, go for a more basic approach. One way to test the effect of your sound bite is to try it out on members of your inner circle.

THE COMMERCIAL

The commercial is a longer version of the sound bite and can be used in networking situations in which you have more time to talk about yourself, such as when you are having lunch with a contact or visiting in her office. It's also a good response when you're conducting an informational interview and the interviewee turns the tables and starts asking questions about you. The commercial can also piggyback on top of the sound bite; you start out with the sound bite, and your conversation partner asks you to tell more about yourself, so you segue into the commercial. This introduction is typically thirty to sixty seconds long and contains more about your background, qualifications, and skills than the sound bite does. Obviously, you don't want your commercial to sound memorized. But you are, after all, talking about yourself, so the material should not be hard to remember. It helps to write it out first (outline form is fine), then read it over a few times, and practice saying it without reading or memorizing it. It's not a big deal if you forget a detail, as long as you remember the main points you want to get across. Here are a couple of samples:

"Hi, my name is Michaela Shaw. In my job as database controller for _____ company, where I worked for ___ years, I was drawn to the field of information systems. I enjoyed the challenge of learning new technologies, and I loved implementing the systems management training I received while working with the Hewlett-Packard board test system. It was as if a spark ignited and suddenly I knew what I wanted to do. I began to focus my efforts on obtaining additional training in computer information systems. In my _____ classes, I led a research team in ___ subject, and . . . (other experience). My academic work has strengthened my communications skills, which were extremely important in my job as _____. I have also worked with the latest technologies in my classes. For example, I helped design a database interface application in Visual Basic for one of my school's programs. Whenever I have been assigned a project, I have done my best to see it through to top-notch completion. I am prepared to take the next step in my career."

"Hi, my name is Mateo Santiago. My background to date has centered around preparing myself to be the most well-rounded marketing professional possible. I have specifically prepared myself for a career in marketing by taking competitive undergraduate classes and by gaining invaluable real-world experience. To improve my written communication skills, I completed four upper-division English classes in addition to the two core classes required of business majors. Since many Texas businesses work with people of Hispanic origin, I chose to enhance my desirability and versatility as a potential employee by acquiring a Spanish minor. I have also acquired real-world experience to prepare myself for the business world, including travel abroad, internships, and entrepreneurial opportunities. While interning with a private organization in Ecuador this past summer, I developed a fifteen-page marketing plan, composed in Spanish, that recommended more effective ways in which this company could promote its services. I also traveled abroad on two other occasions in which I researched the indigenous culture of the Mayan Indians in Todos Santos, Guatemala, and participated in a total language immersion program in San José, Costa Rica. In addition to my travel and internship experience, I also obtained considerable professional sales training as a result of my own entrepreneurial pursuits. During this past summer, I telemarketed for Riella Tire Supply of West Texas, a work experience that prompted me to develop my conflict-resolution and personal selling skills. Furthermore, I have established and maintained two businesses—Santiago Lawn Service and Full Throttle Auto Detailing, which gave me useful real-world experience with cold door-to-door sales calls and relationship selling. As you can see, I am committed to succeed as a marketing professional."

THE INFOMERCIAL

The infomercial is meant for extended networking situations where you are spending a significant chunk of time with a contact. Perhaps you hit it off with someone in your field on a five-hour cross-country airplane flight. Or you are rooming with a stranger at a professional conference who promises to be a helpful contact. The infomercial may not come into play very often, but when it does, you have the opportunity to really sell yourself. The infomercial builds on the commercial. Instead of extending your commercial sales pitch, however, the infomercial consists primarily of preparing for questions your networking partner is likely to pose after hearing about your background. The truly interested and invested network contact asks these questions so that she can better assist you. Among the questions you should be prepared to respond to as part of your Infomercial:

- How did you get into this field?
- How would you describe your ideal job?
- What goals do you have for five years from now?
- What are your strengths and weaknesses?
- Do you plan to obtain further education or training in pursuit of your goals?
- In what geographic area do you want to work?

Your infomercial presentation can also include your observations about interesting trends and events in your field.

PROMOTIONAL TOOLS THAT GREASE THE NETWORKING WHEELS

For truly successful networking, the pearls of wisdom that tumble from your mouth when you talk to people are best accompanied by the printed word. Think of these tools as the promotional literature that help you sell the product. Most importantly, don't go anywhere without your resume and business cards!

RESUME

Always keep your resume updated, and always keep copies in a place where you can easily access them. A slim portfolio that you carry with you is best. Your briefcase is also a possibility, although you may not be carrying it everywhere you go. If in no other place, at least keep some copies handy in your car so you can fetch them when the occasion arises. Make sure the

FOOT | NOTE

Whether using the verbal or written tools of networking, you'll make a lasting impression on your contacts if you are passionate about your field and the job you hope to attain.

copies are clean and crisp, not tattered or dog-eared. For networking, it's especially important to have as much information as possible on your resume about how to contact you. Your resume has a twofold purpose when you're networking. You can give it out when people ask for it or when you otherwise sense an opportunity. But you can also ask your contacts for advice about it. Often they will want you to leave it with them so that they can take time to digest it and formulate suggestions. The result is that you will have not only obtained a critique but also given your contact a "leave-behind" containing all your information. Whenever you feel it's appropriate, ask your contacts if they'd like extra copies of your resume to distribute to others.

BUSINESS CARD

Always keep a plentiful supply of updated business cards with you whenever you network. They are the stock-in-trade of networking. But what if you're currently unemployed or are a not-yet-employed college student? In that case, use a networking card.

NETWORKING CARD

A networking card is exactly like a business card, but for people not currently employed. It contains all the information about how to contact you. Instead of listing your job title and where you work, it lists your area of expertise and/or what you have to offer. You can order networking cards from a printer or office-supply company just as you would order business cards, but it's easy to make networking cards inexpensively on your own. Most office supply stores sell $8\frac{1}{2}$-x-11-inch sheets of business-card stock in various colors and designs (you can even get cardstock that matches your resume). They are designed to be printed on your laser or inkjet printer. To

FOOT   NOTE

Don't be afraid to get creative with printed pieces you hand out when you're networking. Consider the impact a colorful brochure or newsletter about you might have on your contacts.

set them up on your computer, try using the template function of your word-processing program. When they come out of the printer, you separate the cards at the perforations, and voilá—networking cards. Here's a sample of what a networking card might look like:

Web page: www.snicker.com/~acosta/index.html

KATE ACOSTA
Systems Analyst

Product rollout and expansion strategist with heavy network systems connectivity experience.

717-555-1939

E-mail: kacosta@hotmail.com

Fax: 717-555-1861

RESUME HIGHLIGHTS CARD

To take your business or networking card to the next level, you can have highlights from your resume printed on the back of it. The card is useful for times when it would be awkward or inappropriate to distribute your resume. Obviously, you can't fit your whole resume on the back of a card, but you can fit a key word, skills, or qualifications summary. The resume highlights card might look something like this:

QUALIFICATIONS SUMMARY

Business-partnership development.

Corporate image enhancement.

Business structure experience.

E-commerce expertise.

PERSONAL WEB SITE

A Web site, of course, is not a printed item, and you're not about to go around giving out printouts of your Web page. Yet, a personal Web site can be an excellent networking tool. If you have your own Web site, you can keep your updated resume on it, along with links to samples of your work—writing samples, business plans, projects, and designs. A number of Internet service providers offer free space on Web; see the Resources section for how to find free Web space. Let's look at a scenario in which the Web page might come into play:

> *You, on the phone with a prospective network contact:* Hello, Mr. Marks, my name is Tom Butler. Peggy Freedman suggested that you would be a great person to talk with about the publishing field. I'm an English teacher considering a move into that field and I wondered if I could have a few moments of your time to talk about it.
>
> *Mr. Marks:* Sure, that would be fine. It would help a lot, though, if I could see your resume. I think I could be more helpful if I know more about your background. Can you mail or fax me a copy?
>
> *You:* I think I can get my resume in front of you even faster, Mr. Marks. Do you have access to the Web?
>
> *Mr. Marks:* Yes.
>
> *You:* My resume can be viewed on my Web page at *www.plex.com/butler_resume.html*. The Web page also has links to writing samples so you can get a better idea of my abilities.
>
> *Mr. Marks:* That's great! I'll look it over and give you a call back later this afternoon with some suggestions.

If you have a Web site, be sure its address appears on all your printed materials, too.

Chapter Twelve

HOW NETWORKING REALLY WORKS:
A WEEK IN THE LIFE OF A NETWORKER

To illustrate how networking really works and show what wording your letters and phone calls might contain, let's look back at our friend John from Chapter 1, the systems analyst ready to change careers. John had the opportunity to teach a class in systems analysis one semester at a community college, and he discovered that he especially enjoyed designing the curriculum. He got a kick out of planning his syllabus and setting up his entire course on a Web site. He decided that instructional design was a field he'd really like to get into, especially since he was weary of his current career. As Guy Felton suggests on his networking Web site, John made it clear to each contact exactly what he was asking for, and those requests are indicated in bold in the following. Here's how John's first week of networking went:

MONDAY

After work, John attends a meeting of the Association of Instructional Designers. During the social hour, John mingles with the instructional design professionals, using the sound bite technique:

> "Hi, my name is John Randall. I'm a systems analyst, but I'm really interested in getting into your field."

John goes on to describe how much he'd enjoyed designing his own course and how he feels his current career relates to instructional design. John also asks questions about his contacts' jobs—how they got into the field, what they enjoy about it, what exactly their role is. He asks open-ended questions to keep the conversation flowing. Almost everyone John talks to is friendly and receptive and offers him a business card (and John asks for one if a contact neglects to offer him a card). He closes several conversations by asking **who else he should be talking to about getting into the field** and jots down several names. By the end of the evening, he has a good feel for the key area employers in the instructional design field, and he also asks his contacts for **the names of key people at those companies.**

TUESDAY

John organizes the business cards and list of names he's collected from the meeting. The first person he calls is Della, who seemed particularly friendly and interested in helping John break into instructional design. John begins the conversation like this:

> "Hi, this is John Randall. I met you at the meeting of the Association of Instructional Designers last night and really enjoyed talking with you and hearing your advice. Do you have a few minutes? [Waits for response.] As you may recall, I'm interested in breaking into instructional design and would love to get together with you briefly and hear some more of that great advice." (John is careful to tell everyone with whom he tries to arrange a meeting that he needs only a few minutes of their time, but he's also poised to ask questions over the phone in case the contact can't spare time for a one-on-one meeting.)

Della suggests that they meet for coffee the next day. John plans for his face-to-face meeting with Della (and the other meetings he will have in the future) by coming up with some questions he wants to ask. (The list of two hundred questions for informational interviews, especially those in the "Seeking General Advice and Referrals from Your Interviewee" and "Seeking Advice If You Are a Career Changer" sections in Chapter 20, is a good place to begin.) Later, John looks at his list of people whom organization members suggested he contact. Since he hasn't met any of these people, he decides it might be a good idea to write to some of them to introduce himself before calling.

(The letter on the next page is a good example of the standard business-letter format. Other sample letters in the book are examples of content only, not format. Refer back to this example if you need to know how to set up your letter.)

John H. Randall
1545 Elmont Street
Kansas City, MO 64114
(816) 555-3829

November 30, 2000

Mr. C. Benjamin Stevenson
Curriculum Design Dept.
InstructoSource
555 Fifth Avenue
Kansas City, MO 64100

Dear Mr. Stevenson:

Barry Bartram, whom I met at a recent meeting of the Association of
Instructional Designers, suggested I contact you about my interest in
entering the instructional design field. I'm currently a systems analyst,
but I did some instructional design as the result of teaching a class at
Indian Mills Community College. I am extremely intrigued by the
field, especially the possibilities that Web-based instruction presents.

I would be very grateful for any suggestions you might have.

I'd like to contact you in the near future to "pick your brain."
I won't take much of your time and will greatly appreciate any advice
you can offer.

Sincerely,

John Randall

John Randall

WEDNESDAY

John has his meeting with Della over coffee. She is just as congenial as she was Monday night. She suggests a couple of courses that John might take to bolster his instructional design skills, and she gives him some additional names of people to contact. **John has brought some copies of his resume and tells Della to feel free to distribute them to appropriate contacts in her network.** John also asks Della to keep him in mind if she hears of any appropriate job leads for him. Della reveals that she is close friends with a hiring manager at one of the companies John is interested in. **He asks Della for a direct introduction to the hiring manager** and Della says she'll see what she can do. As a next step, John tells Della that he will follow up on her suggestions and will let her know next week how things are going. John goes home to write more letters and phone people on his growing list of contacts. Some of the people he calls agree to meet with him; others give him still more names. In the course of one conversation, John discovers a mutual interest in golf with his contact, Greg, who invites John to play a round the following Sunday. John also takes some time on Wednesday to write a thank-you note to Della (see Part 4). He tucks a magazine article that he thinks would interest Della into the envelope.

THURSDAY

John has lunch with his good friend, Sid, a member of his inner circle. John tells Sid about his plans to change careers and about his networking efforts. It turns out that Sid knows someone in a management position at a software company that often hires instructional designers. Sid gives John contact information for his friend, Dave. **John asks if Sid can "pre-sell" him to Dave before John contacts Dave.** Sid gets out his cell phone, calls Dave right away, and sings John's praises. Dave tells Sid that John should call him at home that evening. He begins the conversation like this:

> "Hi, my name is John Randall. Sid Jackson suggested I contact you. Have I caught you at a good time? [Waits for response.] I'm exploring the instructional design field, and Sid tells me that your company has an instructional design component. I'm not

quite at the point of looking for a job in the field, but I wondered if I could snag a few minutes of your time so that I could tell you what I'm doing, ask you a few questions about your company, and get your perspective on what it takes to be an instructional designer."

Dave invites John to come to his office the next week. John immediately calls Sid to tell him about the successful conversation he had with Dave and to thank Sid for the productive referral.

FRIDAY

John figures that Mr. Stevenson, the referral he wrote to on Tuesday, has probably received his letter by now, so it's time to follow up with a phone call. He begins the conversation like this:

"Hi, Mr. Stevenson, this is John Randall calling. I wrote you a letter earlier this week. Am I keeping you from anything? [Waits for response.] As you recall, I wrote to see if I could get your advice about getting into the instructional design field. Do you have any suggestions for me?"

Mr. Stevenson explains that he does not have time for a meeting, but John is ready with a few quick questions to ask over the phone. Mr. Stevenson suggests a number of companies that John should consider, and he also gives John several more names. After hanging up, John writes Mr. Stevenson a thank-you note and strategizes about how he will contact his new referrals. Figuring that he might be able to get his feet wet in the field by taking on an instructional-design project on a consulting basis, **John plans to ask some of them if they know of any new projects in instructional design or problems that firms in the field may be experiencing.**

SATURDAY

John spends some time organizing his networking information and growing set of contacts. He makes plans for the following week's networking activities. John also uses his downtime on Saturday to read trade publications in the instructional design field, as well as current business publications. He knows that keeping current on developments in the field will help grease the wheels of his conversations with contacts, and the tidbits he picks up from business publications will enable him to offer timely insights and ideas to the people he talks to—so that his encounters aren't totally one-sided.

SUNDAY

John enjoys his golf game with Greg. The hours on the golf course enable John to get to know Greg better and obtain significant advice from him. He also gets some new referral names from Greg. **He asks Greg which executive recruiters are used by the companies John is most interested in and Greg fills him in.** John's networking thus far has yielded the information that a key vice president in the instructional-design field is also a golfer, and **John asks Greg if Greg knows where the vice president plays golf, and Greg tells him.** After returning home, John writes Greg a thank-you letter and offers to host Greg at his local golf course soon. John makes plans to play a round at the club the target vice president uses in the hope John can talk to him there.

By Sunday night, John is beginning to realize, thanks to the advice of the many people he's talked to over the last week, that he will probably need to obtain a little more training before he can make the transition into instructional design. He knows, however, that his network is well established and that he can continue to build on it while keeping his current job and taking some night courses. He makes plans to get back in touch with all the people who have given him advice to update them on his progress and see if they have any further suggestions. He is looking forward to his meeting with Sid's friend, Dave, in the coming week. **John plans to ask Dave for advice on how to approach Dave's company, which is one of John's targeted employers.**

Thus, we've seen through John's experience that networking is especially effective when you ask clearly for what you want each contact to do for you. Among the specifics you can ask for:

- Distribution of your resume to appropriate contacts
- Names of key people at targeted employers
- Advice on how to approach a targeted employer
- A direct introduction to a hiring manager
- Having a contact pave the way or "pre-sell" you to a key person
- Information about new projects you might be able to tackle and problems you might be able to solve at targeted companies
- Information on where a key person plays golf or otherwise spends his leisure time
- Information on which executive recruiters key companies employ

25 LITTLE-KNOWN NETWORKING TIPS

1. *Christmas can be a jolly time to network.*

   Everyone knows that no one hires during the Christmas holidays, so it must therefore be a terrible time to network, right? Wrong. Christmas can be an excellent time to network. Why? Consider the following:

   - According to the U.S. Department of Labor, December, January, and February are actually the three best hiring months. Thus, holiday networking is well timed to pay off by the first of the new year.
   - Since most people assume the winter holidays are terrible for job seeking, you will have less competition than at other times. Legions of workers wait until January to seek a new job for the same reason that people wait until the new year to lose weight—they want to get a fresh start.
   - Lots of parties are held during the holidays. These soirees can provide wonderful opportunities to network in a festive and relaxed setting. The generosity of spirit that marks the season may help put managers into a hiring mood.
   - Those with hiring power are less likely to travel over the holidays, so they are more accessible.
   - At Christmastime, you often see contacts you haven't seen in awhile. Many high schools hold class reunions during the Thanksgiving and Christmas holidays.

2. *So can summer.*

   Similarly, summer can be a great time to network. Competition is minimal because job seekers assume that hiring decisions will be postponed until fall. While the assumption often proves correct, the groundwork for hiring can be laid in the summer—through effective networking. Just as parties and networking opportunities increase during the Christmas holidays, picnics, barbecues, beach parties, and outdoor sporting activities provide sizzling summertime networking occasions. Vacations can be planned around the possibility of relocating to another city. In addition, fiscal years often begin in June or July, making new hiring possible.

3. *Keep networking after your job offer.*

   What would you do if you suddenly lost your job and were not permitted to take your Rolodex or computerized database of your contacts because they were considered company property? Such an abrupt cutoff from one's network is not uncommon, and it makes clear the importance of continuous networking even when you're employed. If you've landed a job as the result of networking, don't abandon your circle of contacts just because you've now got a job. In fact, you may find members of your network more receptive to you when you're employed than when you're out of work. And be sure to keep your own personal records of contact information—perhaps in more than one location—so that your lifeline won't be cut off if your employer takes away access to your computer, databases, and other files.

4. *Networking within your own company is a smart move.*

   By no means should you limit networking-while-employed to external contacts. Building a network within your company not only enhances your prospects for promotion but provides that extra bit of insurance in

FOOT NOTE

Your internal networking efforts can really pay off if a merger causes significant numbers of your colleagues to lose their jobs. As they take new jobs, you'll add new dimensions to your network—contacts in lots of companies where you didn't have contacts before.

case things don't work out in your current position. Periodically evaluate your collegiality with your supervisors, subordinates, and co-workers to see where you stand. Would they help you if you no longer worked at the company? Reinforce any bonds that seem weak. Writing for the National Association for Female Executives, Inc., George Tunick recommends that you "volunteer for team projects, help people who have been appointed to committees or special projects, and attend all corporate social events." Don't forget that while your peers might seem like competition, any one of them could be your boss someday, whether in this company or another. If a major downsizing hit your company, and one of your co-workers quickly gained a job with hiring power, would you be one of the first people he or she would think of hiring? No? Better put some energy into that on-the-job networking! As Tunick writes, "Networking within your company gives you access to the informal grapevine and a better understanding of the unwritten rules that each company follows. Close friends at the office can help educate you, provide moral and emotional support during down periods, and defend you when you need it. Also, your allies spread the word about you. Your internal group can promote your talents and special abilities so that others in your company recognize your competence."

5. *"Alliancing" is networking's next frontier.*

   Alliancing is the next level in networking within one's company. The term was coined by management psychologist Carol A. Gallagher, who describes alliancing as "developing close ties with top executives above the glass ceiling and good working relationships with peers," and calls such affiliations "instrumental in helping them [employees] gain access to the company's more prestigious jobs." This practice of forging strategic partnerships is particularly helpful to those—often women—for whom traditional networking in the traditional "old boy" style has not been effective. Targets for these strategic alliances are typically immediate supervisors and others at the next level of the corporate hierarchy. These are the people who can best champion your promotability when you perform well and demonstrate loyalty. Close collaboration on projects and weathering crises together are the hallmarks of alliancing.

When you serve not only as an invaluable right-hand person to your supervisor, but also as an eager protégé, you set yourself up not only for promotion but as the person most likely to be hired in your boss's place if he or she takes a job elsewhere. A terrific side benefit is the enhanced job satisfaction you gain from your outstanding synergy with your boss.

6. *The open job market can be networked, too.*

Just because most job vacancies aren't advertised, and most successful candidates find jobs through methods other than responding to classified ads, doesn't mean that networking is incompatible with answering want ads. In fact, combining networking with responding to ads makes for a potent blend of techniques. Networking reinforces your ad-response efforts. You could, for example, hand-deliver your resume and cover letter in response to an ad on the off chance you'll get to meet someone with hiring power. You probably won't, and you shouldn't push for a meeting, but at the very least, you've made an impression—favorable, we hope—on the gatekeeper (secretary, receptionist, or assistant) who took

FOOT NOTE

Self-promotion is important when you're "alliancing" or networking within your own company. Make sure the right people know what you're doing, advises Michelle Woodward. Writing for *womenCONNECT.com*, Woodward tells of watching an equally qualified colleague with less seniority get promoted over her. The colleague knew how to network the right people with phone contacts, memos, and personal visits. Woodward's suggestions:

- **Know who really has the power to promote you, and make sure your networking efforts familiarize that person with your work.**
- **In meetings, give bullet points that describe your projects.**
- **Teamwork is great, but don't be afraid to say "I," instead of "we," sometimes.**
- **Send e-mail messages to your supervisor describing activities and accomplishments. (My college professor husband is a big proponent of this technique; he sends the dean a monthly e-mail listing his achievements.)**

your material from you. Networking can be effectively utilized within your job-search correspondence itself. If your networking efforts coincide with an advertised vacancy, you can mention a referral in your cover letter—perhaps a mutual acquaintance. This technique is discussed in greater detail in Chapter 24. The most common way to combine networking with responding to ads is to follow up on your job-search correspondence, using methods described in Part 4. The bottom line here is that even though networking is an extremely important component of job hunting, you should not place all your eggs in the networking basket. For best results, use networking in combination with conventional job-hunting methods on both the open and closed markets.

7. *Open yourself to unexpected opportunities.*

Networking opportunities frequently present themselves when you don't consider yourself to be in networking mode, or when you're attending an event that you don't think of as a networking venue. "It seems as if my best networking occurs when I'm least expecting it or putting any focus into it," observes Wendy Gordy, career services coordinator at the University of Kansas. The very improbability of making good contacts in certain situations sometimes actually fosters networking, as Joanna Davis, associate director in a college student services office, found out. During a road rally in Hawaii, "I happened to be assigned to share a car with the president of a large international company," Davis relates. "The road rally consisted of driving from point to point on the island and taking 'creative photographs' with your vehicle's passengers. This 'silliness' created a sense of rapport that facilitated a networking conversation."

Martha Boerema, associate career center director at a major university, notes that her greatest opportunities have come "at points in my life when I was ready to recognize an opportunity, but not actively seeking a change." Sometimes chance occurrences or overheard conversations result in networking opportunities. Sandra Grabczynski, a director of employer development and relations, remembers the time a business plan was sent to her by mistake. "I read the plan and was so interested in the nature of the business, I called the vice president [of the business] directly to discuss my skills," she recalls. "Three months later I was employed full-time with them." Maureen Pernick, director of cooperative education and career development for a private college, once overheard a conversation between two of her friends in which one was telling the other about a job she had heard about but didn't interest her. Pernick, however, was interested. She obtained more information, applied for the job, and got it.

Be prepared for those unexpected opportunities by always carrying copies of your resume with you, along with a business card or networking card.

8. *Network "above your station."*
   Ever hear the adage about how you should dress, not like other people at your own level, but like those at the level you aspire to? The same applies to networking—at least to some degree. You will often learn the most and make the best connections, not with your peers, but with those at higher levels. Certainly you should not ignore the members of your own cohort, but be sure to include in your network a healthy number of folks who are in the kind of job you hope to achieve someday.

9. *Getting on board: Joining boards is a great way to network.*
   At some point in your career, you may be asked to participate on a corporate or nonprofit board, either in a decision-making or advisory capacity. Membership on some boards is by application rather than invitation; check into boards associated with your local government, for example. My county government in Volusia County, Florida, has several dozen advisory boards open to local residents—from the Commission on the Status of Women to the Cultural Arts Advisory Board. Although board membership is a serious responsibility and time commitment (boards generally meet anywhere from four to twelve times per year), it can be a rewarding networking opportunity because of the accompanying clout and prestige. Board membership frequently affords you the chance to rub elbows with some of the most powerful members of the community or corporate world—people you might not normally get to meet. To maximize the opportunity, don't just sit there at meetings and

say "yea" or "nay"; get actively involved. Volunteer for committees. The more you do for the board, the more people of influence you'll be able to network with.

10. *Get yourself on headhunters' A-lists.*

Headhunters, or as they are more properly known, executive recruiters, work for client employers, so we don't think of them as being especially approachable by job hunters for networking. Yet, you can build relationships with headhunters by serving as a source for them, especially if your own career is at the executive level. Executive recruiters are always on the lookout for talented people to fill positions at client companies. If you can steer good people toward your favorite headhunter, you may be favorably remembered when it's time for your own job search. Similarly, helping a headhunter find clients or serving as a client yourself will stand you in good stead with the recruiter, who will undoubtedly be eager to repay the favor when you need help with your job search.

11. *Recruiters network, too, and you can take advantage.*

Executive recruiting is largely a word-of-mouth business. Recruiters find out about top people to recruit for their client companies essentially through networking. Therefore, the more you network, the more you let people know what you're in the market for, and the more you present yourself as a dynamic, can-do professional, the more likely it is that recruiters will hear of your reputation and give you a call. If you've

The Nitty-Gritty

FOOT NOTE

Don't know how to locate headhunters (executive recruiters)? Contact the Recruiting & Search Report (904-235-3733) for its inexpensive directories covering 5,600 headhunters classified by industry/functional specialty. Consultant News (603-585-2200) publishes annual editions of *The Directory of Executive Recruiters*, which is available in bookstores or from the publisher.

established a relationship with an executive recruiter, make sure he or she knows about every move you make. Keep in touch anytime you get a new job or promotion.

12. *Find a mentor, the ultimate network contact.*

If you do no other kind of networking, at least find yourself a mentor—or let one find you. A mentor is that one person who can guide you, help you, take you under his or her wing, and nurture your career quest. A Yoda to your Luke Skywalker. A Glinda the Good Witch to your Dorothy Gale. What separates a mentor from the average network contact is long-term commitment and a deep-seated investment in your future. Where a typical network contact might be associated with quick introductions, exchanges of business cards, and phone calls, your relationship with a mentor is likely to involve long lunches and meetings in the mentor's office. A mentor is often in a position you'd like to be in and has the clout and connections to guide you to a similar position. She is probably someone with whom you have unusually good chemistry, and who will share stories with you of his or her own climb to success. An effective mentor isn't afraid to criticize constructively.

To find a mentor, identify someone you admire, and test the waters by asking for advice. Be sure to reveal as much of your personality, experience, and goals as possible. Mentors are most likely to invest themselves in people who remind them a little of themselves, which is why you should never approach a prospective mentor in a state of desperation or helplessness. The mentor wants to work with someone he or she

FOOT NOTE

For a comprehensive source on finding and benefiting from mentors, see The Directory of Mentor Arts and Mentorship at *http://www.peer.ca/mentor.html*. A particularly valuable resource for women on making the most of a mentoring relationship is the 1999 book by Carolyn Duff, *Learning from Other Women: How to Benefit from Knowledge, Wisdom and Experience of Female Mentors* (Amacom).

can respect. He may even desire to mold the protégé in his or her own image; this type of relationship will work as long as the mentor is not too obsessive about it and you are comfortable with the image into which you're being molded. You should have a good feel after a few meetings as to whether the rapport is right for a mentoring relationship. At that point, you can either come right out and ask the person to be your mentor, if that feels appropriate, or you can simply tell him or her how much you've benefited from the advice you've received so far and that you hope he or she will continue to share it with you. Although the mentor will tend to give a lot more than you do to the relationship, be sure to express regularly that you value and appreciate the mentor's guidance. The feeling of being needed and making a difference in a protégé's life will often be a rewarding payoff for the mentor.

Sometimes the very act of seeking a mentor can become its own networking experience, as it did for Nancy DeCrescenzo, director of a career counseling office. "An interviewer suggested I get a mentor in higher education, the field I was interested in entering," DeCrescenzo recalls. "I visited my local community college, knocked on the door of Career Services and asked the friendly guy in the office for help. He referred me to the director of career counseling at another nearby school, who in turn shared a copy of a networking newsletter that contained the posting for the position I now hold. It was a bold course of action for a frustrated job seeker that really paid off!"

13. *Capitalize on gender differences when networking.*

Who are the more successful networkers, men or women? You might guess women because women seem like the natural talkers, while we tend to think of men as holding back. The facts indicate that men use networking more effectively than women, however. The results of a 1997 study conducted by EnterChange, an outplacement and career management consulting firm, and reported by Valerie Frazee in *Workforce* magazine, show, for example, that women are more likely than men to find their next job through an ad in the classifieds, while networking is a more effective strategy for men than women. Does that mean that women should put down this book and go start scouring the classifieds? Or that men don't even need this book? No. It just means that men and women should use their different styles to greatest advantage. Consider the following:

Women's networks tend to be more egalitarian and inclusive than men's, according to writer Kathy Harvey, who describes a career consulting company's experience with asking women to list people who might form part of their network. Women were more likely to mention people at lower levels than themselves (along with those in the higher echelons), while men tended to focus on people with power and influence. Men may benefit from network contacts with greater clout, but women can take advantage of wider and more diverse circles of contacts. Some experts also say women are better at sharing than men, so both men and women may be able to expect more career-based generosity from female members of their networks than either gender can from men.

Men are said to have built-in networks, often referred to as "old boy" networks. One reason men's networks include the powerful and influential is the simple truth that the contacts with the most clout are still most likely to be men. In other words, a guy's fraternity brother from college is more likely to be a CEO than a woman's sorority sister is—hence, the built-in network that men can capitalize on.

Women have traditionally been expected to devote more time to family and domestic responsibilities, thus having less time than men to build networks. We're starting to see more women networking out there on the golf course, for instance, but that's a fairly new phenomenon. To be truly competitive in the networking arena, women may have to put more time into making contacts—and they may have to ask their male partners to take on a bigger share in managing family life.

The number of all-women networking groups is increasing enormously, with the intent, in part, to create the same kind of networks that are already entrenched for men. An all-women networking group can be very beneficial to young women seeking mentors and contacts who've already succeeded in breaking through the glass ceiling. These groups also can be an efficient way to deal with the time crunch that too often curtails women's networking.

14. *Use networking to show your "fit" with the job.*

Have you ever noticed that certain professions seem to evoke images of specific kinds of personalities? We think, for example, of bankers and lawyers as being somewhat conservative, morticians as solemn, and salespeople, publicists, and those in the hospitality industry as extremely outgoing and bubbly. While some images are pure stereotype, certain personalities really do match professions because particular characteristics are required for success in those fields. If you're in sales or marketing, for example, you truly do need exceptional warmth, effusiveness, and interpersonal skills. You need to be able to schmooze. Thus, when you network in the field you hope to break into (or advance in), it only makes sense to project the right kind of personality for the kind of job you seek. Ideally, you want the contacts you meet to think to themselves, "Wow, she would be great as a [fill in the name of your dream job here]." This advice might seem a little too obvious; of course you'll project the right kind of personality when you network. If you didn't, you wouldn't be in the right line of work. But be forewarned: First, if it doesn't feel comfortable to you to "play the game" the way others in your field do, maybe you really should be questioning your career choice. And second, remember that you have to put that game face on whenever you network. If a protracted job search has got you in a funk, it may be best to pass up a few networking opportunities until you're in a more appropriate frame of mind.

15. *Choose the right networking style by learning how to read people.*

You can enhance your networking success by learning to read people's individual styles—and by subtly mirroring those styles. It's a time-honored technique used in sales: The salesperson does as much as possible to match the style of the prospective customer. The result can be chemistry or rapport that increases the possibility of making the sale. In his book, *College Grad Job Hunter*, Brian Krueger calls this method the Personality Matching Technique and suggests applying it in job interviews. If you match your voice pitch, speaking tempo, facial expressions, and posture with those of your interviewer, you will increase the interviewer's comfort level with you, Krueger asserts. Of course, you don't want to seem as though you are mimicking the other person. But if you can, for example, speak at the same pace as the person you're talking to, you'll seem to be similar in style, and that person will perceive you as a good fit with the team. You can do the same thing with the people you network with. Adapt your style or approach to theirs, and they will be more likely to include you in their circle and help you in your job search.

Writer Iris Randall divides businesspeople into "Directors," "Influencers," "Steadiers," and "Conscientious Thinkers," suggesting that once you identify which type you are encountering, you can then network with each one in his or her own style. Directors, Randall says, are CEO types who thrive on being in charge. They are not into details, and they like very direct responses to their questions. Salespeople are the best example of Influencers. Relationships are what light their fires, so the best way to an Influencer's heart is to discuss mutual acquaintances. Steadiers are splendid team players and conflict resolvers who may respond by playing a counselor role when you network with them. Conscientious Thinkers are logical and analytical. Randall suggests that the Conscientious Thinker is the type with whom you'll get the best results if you leave a resume and then follow up with a phone call.

16. *Show—don't just tell.*

As you're networking, don't just tell your contacts about your skills and talents, demonstrate them, too. When it comes to successful networking, "it's not who you know, it's what you show that counts," write Julie Finley and Tom Unger in *Communication World.* You especially have the opportunity to show what you can do within professional and volunteer groups. Finley and Unger recommend signing up for your organization's awards committee, helping to plan meetings and events, publicizing the association, developing surveys, or editing the group's newsletter or other publications—including on-line publications, such as a Web site. College instructor Karen Baker relates how demonstrating her skills helped her network. "As a result of an Internet study I completed and presented at a national conference, one of my study participants approached me after the session," Baker recalls. "She complimented the study and presentation; we talked a bit about what she did, what my plans were, and exchanged business cards. A few months later, a faculty position became available at her school, and she was chairing the search committee. When I sent my credentials, I reminded her of our meeting. I ended up being offered the position."

17. *Speak the language.*

An easy way to gain a psychological edge in the networking world is to learn the jargon of the industry you seek to enter or advance in. Skillfully using the lingo of the profession makes you seem like an insider as you connect with people "in the biz." Reading professional publications related to your field will help you pick up terms, as will conducting informational interviews (see Part 3). "Continually updating professional language is a key indicator of dedication and interest in a particular field," writes Mickey Veich in *Security Management* magazine.

18. *College students can parlay summer jobs into networking opportunities.*

College students are often dismayed when they have to settle for humbling summer jobs unrelated to the field they hope to enter after graduation. But every summer job, no matter how seemingly menial, can be a networking opportunity. A summer job provides a chance to sharpen your work ethic, learn as much as you can, and network, network, network. Choose a service job at a resort or theme park, for example, and you can find yourself hobnobbing with successful people from all over the world. Not every summer job will be that exotic, but those that offer the best networking opportunities engender plenty of contact with people. Whether you're a receptionist, a server in a restaurant, or a sales associate in a department store, every personal encounter with customers and co-workers is a networking opportunity. Be friendly, strike up conversations at appropriate moments, and let folks know of your career interests. When you come across someone who seems as though she can be especially helpful, try to obtain a business card or contact information. Later, when you're back in school, contact your most promising summer acquaintances and ask them to become part of your network. Include your summer-job supervisors in that network, too.

19. *Temporary work is a great arena for networking.*

If you're ever in a transitional period in which you are not working in your career field, working through a temporary employment agency can be an excellent networking opportunity. When you work for a temp agency, you are assigned to do various kinds of work at client companies for varying lengths of time—a few days, a couple of weeks, several months, or longer. The skills needed vary, but a temp worker's skill set is generally matched with the type of work needed by the client company. Office jobs, for example, require some basic computer/keyboarding skills. The temp agency usually evaluates those skills with a fairly simple test. Temporary work can even enable you to learn new skills. Training is sometimes available. Temping gives you valuable experience to list on your resume and keeps paychecks coming in as you continue to seek permanent work in your career field. For college students during summer and semester breaks, temping allows valuable opportunities for career exploration. The same applies to career changers. Anyone with uncertainty about what career to move into can expect to find some answers in temping. At the very least, you may learn what fields you don't want to get into. The best temp agencies can also help you with your resume and counsel you about your career.

Best of all, temping is a terrific networking opportunity because you're working not just in one, but in many companies. You rub elbows with all kinds of people who have the opportunity to see what a valuable employee you are. Be prepared to dazzle—or at least meet—as many key people in the client companies as possible: department heads, supervisors, executives, and others with influence. Client companies not only offer the possibility of gaining referrals in your career field, but they can also be an end in themselves. Temp agencies report that some 75 percent of people placed in such assignments are offered full-time jobs, writes Jason Rich, author of *Job Hunting for the Utterly Confused.*

20. *Out of the mouths of babes' parents: Network through your kids.*

Parents who step off the fast track and onto the Mommy or Daddy track tend not to think of preschool, playdates, and "Mommy and Me" classes as good networking opportunities. But because so many young professionals have delayed parenthood and are in the same position, mingling with other parents can be a productive way to make contact. If there's one thing most parents tend to do, it's compare notes. The built-in conversation starter that your kids provide is an excellent launching pad for networking talk. Activities involving your kids even give you the chance to show off some of your professional skills, whether you're organizing a fund-raiser for your childcare cooperative or leading a PTA meeting. Don't be surprised if someday one of the other parents notices your talents and offers to introduce you to a power player or recommend you for an awesome job.

21. *Start a job or networking club.*

An abundance of ready-made networking opportunities exists out there, but maybe none of them are right for you or accessible to you. In that case, form your own. You need only to gather a few friends or acquaintances at someone's house; refreshments are also a nice touch. Your gatherings can be part support group, part think tank. The idea is to share each others' job-hunting and career experiences and encourage each other in the quest. What works? What doesn't? Who's hiring? Who's not? Members should bring resumes, both for critiquing by others in the group and so you can exchange them and distribute members' resumes when opportunities present themselves. Members can also pass out helpful articles about the job search. If you decide to expand— and, for optimal networking, you should—publicize your group in the local paper. If you outgrow people's homes, find a meeting room at the local community hall, church, or restaurant, charging dues to your members, if necessary, to finance the use of the room. The exchange of job leads, business cards, resumes, ideas, and information that occurs in a job or networking club can energize the members and teach everyone valuable career strategies and techniques. Emily Koltnow parlayed the networking group she started into a business. She started a lunch group of six friends who had lost their jobs around the same time Koltnow did, she relates in *Executive Female*. The group soon grew to 261 and ultimately became Women in Networking.

22. *Include the "gatekeepers" in your network.*

Do you consider those pesky secretaries, receptionists, and administrative assistants to be obstacles that keep you from networking with the honchos with the real hiring power? Well, don't. These gatekeepers can be your best friends as you network. In fact, they can be valuable members of your network in their own right. The more you treat them as esteemed network contacts, the more likely they will be to open the gates and put you in touch with their bosses. These folks frequently have their fingers on the pulse of their companies; they, often more than anyone else, know what's going on, who's coming, who's going, and where the openings are likely to be.

Take Maggie Dobson, a gatekeeper at my place of employment, Stetson University. Maggie's title is administrative assistant, but in reality, she is the lifeblood of the university. She knows everything and everyone. Most people predict that the university may fall apart when Maggie retires in a few years. If I were asked who really knows what's going on at Stetson, I'd direct the inquirer to Maggie.

Learn the names of those who stand between you and the higher-ups. We all like to be called by our names, and unless we're frantically busy, we like to be schmoozed. Make friendly conversation with the gatekeepers. Most importantly, ask their advice about how to get your foot in the door of the company. Ask them whom you should be contacting. Thank them profusely when they make suggestions that prove fruitful. Make them feel important—after all, they are.

23. *They'll applaud your brilliance: Speak and write in your area of expertise.*

One of the best ways to get your name into circulation and meet an enormous number of contacts is by writing for local publications and speaking to professional and civic groups. Almost everyone is an expert in some area, and if your area is related to a career field, you can parlay speaking and writing opportunities into your next terrific job. Know a lot about computers? Good at motivating people? Know how to create an effective Web page? Have your finger on the pulse of emerging trends? Groups in your area are always looking for interesting speakers. Obtain lists of local organizations from the library, phone book, chamber of commerce, or newspaper listings of meeting schedules. Call the program chair of, say, a dozen groups, and you'll be amazed how many would love to have you as a speaker—and in the near future to boot. Once you have some speaking engagements lined up, polish your presentation. The more compelling a speaker you are, the better this technique will work. After you've spoken, stick around for the group's social hour. The group's members will be eager to meet you, especially if you've given a fascinating talk. "Automatically the audience is already interested in the topic simply by being present," observes international trade economist Leroy Smith. "This makes the networking activity much easier." Be sure to bring a healthy supply of business cards. You'll make excellent contacts who will see you as more credible than the average Joe Jobseeker, because you've demonstrated your expertise. Jennifer Sumner, an organization development consultant and executive coach for Boeing, scored a networking success when she conducted a personal growth group. "One of the group members encouraged me to talk with the owner of a management consulting firm he used in his business," Sumner remembers. "The firm hired me."

Let groups know that you're also available for panel discussions and roundtables. Any event that increases your visibility can be a terrific networking opportunity. If you have the resources, you can even put on your own workshops and seminars. Contact local colleges and universities to see if they'd be willing to host your presentations. Many schools have continuing-education and Elderhostel programs that are always looking for good instructors.

You can also contact editors of local publications and ask if they could use someone to write a column in your area of expertise. Small weekly newspapers and newsletters are often particularly hungry for this sort of contribution. Publications don't have to be local, either. Trade publications in your field may welcome a column or article of interest to their readerships. This writing effort may not yield a direct networking effect, but it will increase your name recognition and credibility. Ask the editor to run your photo with the column, for even more visibility. You'll introduce yourself to someone during a future networking opportunity and hear them say, "Oh, you write that fascinating column in *The Hometown News*."

The Nitty-Gritty

24. *They'll be watching you: Publicize your every move.*

Any time you make a career move, send out a press release. Initiating this publicity may not seem like networking, but it's a form of indirect networking in that you are increasing your visibility, thus helping your contacts find out where you are and what you're doing. Most local newspapers have a regular column in their business sections precisely for chronicling the career transitions of people like you. Trade publications also frequently have such columns. Your press release should be brief and to the point, and you can get a good idea of how it should be worded by looking at the blurbs in your chosen publications' columns. The release is usually headed with contact information about you in case the editor has any questions, along with the words "FOR IMMEDIATE RELEASE." The release should be double-spaced. Check with the editor about submission preferences; in this electronic age, she might prefer that you submit your release in an e-mail message or as an e-mail attachment. You should also submit a nice photo of yourself, preferably a black-and-white headshot. If you submit your release electronically, you can even scan the photo and send it as an e-mail attachment.

The advantage of this publicity is that it can keep every member of your network informed about what you're up to. As you write regular notes to members of your network, the blurb about your latest move is a perfect piece to clip and send to your contacts, especially those in far-flung locales who may not have seen the item in the publication. Executive recruiters, a.k.a. headhunters, also watch these columns to keep an eye out for promising people they'd like to recruit.

25. *Be a helpful network contact for others.*

Don't forget the old saying, "To have a friend, be a friend." Be as helpful and generous a network contact with others as your contacts have been with you. Always give something to those who seek to include you in their network, whether it is a referral or a word of encouragement. Those you've helped will then be there for you or someone else you know who needs a network contact. You might even want to take your helpfulness to the next level, as Mike Kaplan has. Kaplan, a sales and marketing manager in the technology field, has made career counseling almost a hobby. "The original reason was just to help college students recognize and identify what they want to do," Kaplan relates. "Many of the people I interview for sales positions either have no idea what to expect in a sales job, have expectations that do not make sense, or are using a sales job as an entrance to a company, not as a potential career. As a result of all this, I have been witness to many poor interviews and felt that I have the ability to work with these students to give them an idea of what is really going to happen in an interview. For interested sales people, I can tell them what a sales job is really like."

While the desire to benefit himself played no role in Kaplan's decision to offer help, he recognizes that someday, "theoretically, a student I work with might end up in an influencing position and could help me land a job, close a sale, etc." Helping people in their time of greatest need can pay handsome dividends when those people succeed. Sales and marketing guru Harvey MacKay cautions in his book, *Dig Your Well Before You're Thirsty,* "The bandwagon gets pretty crowded when people realize it's heading toward glory. . . . Don't wait. The time to make your presence felt is when it's just a plain old wagon and no one wants to ride on it."

Chapter Fourteen

NETWORKING IN THE DIVERSE WORK WORLD

The increasing diversity of the workplace mandates a commitment to ethnic and cultural sensitivity, which also applies to networking. Underrepresented groups face special challenges and obstacles in the world of networking. And even those facing no unusual obstacles must be aware of how various groups view networking. One gentleman who wrote to me while I was researching this book pointed out that people of Asian origin tend to look with disdain on the concept of networking because they view the practice as akin to "using" people. An African American woman told me that she has had much networking success in obtaining referrals and interviews but that racism and discrimination had kept her from being hired. While I make no attempt to offer a comprehensive guide to networking for those in underrepresented groups, I offer some tips. Virtually all groups have networking organizations available to them that are specifically earmarked for their situation or ethnicity. Clubs and organizations are available for women, African Americans, Latinos, Asians, the disabled, older workers, and many others, some of which are listed in the Resources

FOOT NOTE

If you're networking in the international arena, be aware that other cultures have different attitudes about networking at social events and business-card exchanges than Americans. Raise your cultural sensitivity by reading up on the customs of other cultures and the acceptability of typically American networking activities. You may even want to take a course or attend a seminar to enhance your awareness of international networking practices.

section. In addition, members of these organizations often particularly benefit from having mentors, especially mentors with the same background. It's always helpful to learn about how someone like you has overcome some of the same obstacles you face. Some additional tips:

• George Fraser is widely regarded as the networking guru for African Americans. Author of *Success Runs in Our Race: The Complete Guide to Networking in the African American Community* and *Race for Success: The Ten Best Business Opportunities for Blacks in America*, Fraser writes, "It is vital for African Americans to network for their common good. In spite of media images to the contrary, we are historically a race of successful people, and we have always been a successful people, even when in chains." Fraser also asserts that most of his ideas on networking for African Americans can also benefit other minority groups. He suggests that members of minority groups must support each other. His advice is helpful not only to members of all underrepresented groups, but to networkers in general.

Fraser and others believe strongly in ethnocentric networks; for African Americans, that means Afrocentric networks, such as churches, which have traditionally helped to hold African American communities together. Another type of Afrocentric group, recommended by Andrea Wright in *Essence* magazine, is the black alumni association. If your school doesn't have one of these associations, consider forming one.

• Groups that are not only Afrocentric but women-centered as well can help African American women's careers. Writing in *Black Enterprise*

FOOT NOTE

George Fraser offers these tips for non–African Americans when they network with blacks:
• Don't generalize about African Americans as a race or assume all have the same tastes; get to know them as individuals.
• Don't assume all 30 million African Americans know each other or have universal knowledge of black popular culture.

magazine (which is another fantastic resource on networking for everyone, not just African Americans), Carolyn Odom Steele declares, "No longer reluctant to leverage our clout or tap into high-powered contacts, these loosely defined, essentially structureless networks are effectively influencing the positions of African American women across the nation." While networking within ethnocentric groups is important, many experts recommend also networking beyond one's own community to expand networking circles.

- Attend black-sponsored events. Invite African Americans—and not just a token few—to attend your events.

- Starting your own networking group (see page 97) can be especially helpful for women, as well as minorities. Women's networking groups have grown significantly in recent years, partly on the theory that women are at their greatest comfort levels when interacting with other women. Communication theorists such as Deborah Tannen (author of *You Just Don't Understand*) suggest that women are better listeners than men; thus, groups providing mutual support work well for women.

- Black fraternities and sororities offer "the post-college networking and support systems that white college graduates have traditionally found in groups like the Jaycees and Kiwanis," writes James Tobin in *The Detroit News*. The major black fraternities are Kappa Alpha Psi, Alpha Phi Alpha, Omega Psi Phi, Phi Beta Sigma, and Iota Phi Theta. The sororities are Alpha Kappa Alpha, Delta Sigma Theta, Zeta Phi Beta, and Sigma Gamma Rho.

FOOT NOTE

iVillage.com (*http://www.ivillage.com/career/*) and Bella-Online (*http://www.bellaonline.com/career/networking_editor_feature.html*) are on-line resources for women that have career and networking advice, as well as chat areas for on-line networking. See Resources section, page 177, for more resources for women.

A FOOT IN THE DOOR

- Don't worry about whether you're bothering people when you network. Columnist Niki Scott encourages women in particular to be persistent, since their natural tendency is to fear that they are annoying people when they seek advice and assistance.

- Learn to play golf. More and more members of underrepresented groups are discovering just how much networking occurs during golf games. "I never thought I would learn to play golf," says University of Central Florida cooperative education coordinator Lara Cegala, "but I have so I could network with employers on the golf course. It's the best way to get their attention."

- Networking is especially important for older workers because jobs at the senior levels are the least likely to be advertised. It's important to fight the perception that your skills and knowledge might not be on the cutting edge. Stay up to date with technological trends and be sure to demonstrate your savvy when you converse with network contacts.

- The AARP, American Association for Retired Persons, offers seminars on post-career planning, workforce reentry, and resume writing for older workers. The seminars provide not only information but networking opportunities. Call the national headquarters at 800-424-3410 (on the Web at *http://www.aarp.org/*) to find out about sessions near you.

- Young networkers should start as early as possible. Always view summer jobs and internships as opportunities to network.

FOOT  NOTE

Among some good networking resources for Hispanics is HispanicBusiness.com (*http://www.HispanicBusiness.com*) which is associated with *Hispanic Business* magazine and offers networking events to the Hispanic community. See Resources section, page 183 for more.

- Tip for former military personnel: Retired military personnel are no strangers to networking, notes Pamela McBride in *Black Enterprise*. It's what they do every day to get things done in the military. While networking comes naturally to former service people, they are accustomed to a sheltered, structured environment. Try to build a civilian network before you leave the service, and don't take rejection personally as you network outside military circles.

- Tip for the downsized or fired worker: Take a little time to step back and decide what you want your next career move to be and what you have to offer when you start networking, advises Ann Meier in *Training & Development*. It's not enough simply to tell the world you're available the moment you're handed that pink slip. You need at least a few days to compose yourself.

Chapter Fifteen

DUCKS IN A ROW:
KEEPING TRACK OF YOUR NETWORK

You can maximize your network's effectiveness if you organize your list of contacts. That way you can keep track of whom you've contacted and when. With a good system, you can have at your fingertips contact names and information that you might otherwise forget. Plan to weed through your organizational system periodically to update contact information and place in an inactive area of your system those members of your network with whom you are no longer in touch.

BUSINESS CARDS

Since business cards are the essential tools of networking, they can also form the basis of an organizational system. At the most rudimentary level, you could simply alphabetize the cards you collect and wrap a rubber band around them. The next step might be purchasing a file box especially made for business cards. You can also buy a Rolodex-type file for business cards, along with a special paper-puncher that punches business cards so they fit easily in a Rolodex.

Some people like to keep their business cards in a binder. If that method appeals to you, you can purchase a business-card binder, which is

FOOT NOTE

When attending network events, use the backs of business cards to jot down information about each person who gave you one. Your notes will help you remember your contacts and enable you to converse intelligently with them the next time you meet.

usually about the size of a business card and fits nicely into an attaché case or purse. If you prefer a three-ring binder, you can get special plastic sheets for business cards. These three-hole-punched, $8\frac{1}{2}$-x-11-inch sheets and can hold ten business cards. Another alternative is to lay ten business cards on the glass of a photocopier in the configuration of an $8\frac{1}{2}$-x-11-inch sheet (two across and five down), photocopy them all onto a page, and three-hole-punch the pages.

ROLODEX SYSTEM

A Rolodex or rotary file is the preferred method of many networkers. Given that you won't always obtain a business card from every contact, a Rolodex system can work well. Information about each person can be written or typed onto Rolodex cards, and for those contacts who do give you business cards, you can staple the cards to the Rolodex cards.

INDEX CARDS

If you desire a system that is as low-tech as a business-card or Rolodex system but that has more space to record information about each contact, you might use file cards, which typically come in 3-x-5-inch, 4-x-6-inch, and 5-x-8-inch sizes, ruled or unruled, and in many colors. File boxes are also available for the cards.

COMPUTERIZED SYSTEMS

Those who prefer a more high-tech system that is easier to update may want to organize their contacts in a spreadsheet program, such as Lotus 1-2-3 or Microsoft Excel. The spreadsheet could have columns for each contact's name, address, phone numbers, fax number, e-mail address, where you met the contact or who referred you, the date you met, your follow-up communications, and comments about the contact and how he or she helped you. See sample spreadsheet entries opposite. You might instead prefer a database program, such as Microsoft Access, Paradox, FileMaker Pro, or Visual FoxPro, which enables you to sort your contacts based on any field of information and to address envelopes or labels if you want to send out mailings to a large number of contacts.

NETWORK CONTACTS

NAME	CO. NAME	TITLE	PHONE	FAX	E-MAIL	HOME PHONE	ADDRESS	COMMENTS
Deborah Mittman	UniSOAR	Mkting Analyst	803/555-9284	803/555-9074	Mitt1@aol.com	803/555-1045	PO Box 1923, Columbia, SC 28540	Met at Conference
Keith Cannon	Barnes & Co.	Mkt. Researcher	843/555-8182	843/555-7734	KC55@yahoo.com	843/555-0092	58 Ross St., Charleston, SC 28540	Very Helpful
Jon Patrick	ReddiNet	VP Marketing	843/555-8763	843/555-0004	jpvp@red.net	843/555-7654	177 3rd Ave., Myrtle Bch, SC 28539	Gave resume critique
Jason Pauls	Taylor Industries	Mkting Director	214/555-6742	214/555.6744	pauls@taylor.com	214.555.2678	1465 Sycamore Ave., Dallas, TX 75260	Deb Mittman's former superviser at UniSOAR
Teresa Vincent	Roderick Ent.	Mkting Analyst	843/555-6914	843/555-6825	tvince@aol.com	843/555-9486	466 Cavour St., Charleston, SC 28540	Granted informational interview

ORGANIZATIONAL SCHEMES

No matter how you choose to record your contacts, you may choose to organize them alphabetically, by the date you met them, by the date of last contact, by city or geographical region, by industry or job type, or by degree of importance or helpfulness to you. Many types of indexes are available for both binder and card systems. Consider whether a system of color coding might be helpful to you. You may want to make a record of each communication you have with a member of your network, along with comments about the encounter. That way you can track who is due for a follow-up, and you can ensure that you don't make a pest of yourself by contacting people too often.

FOOT NOTE

Consider keeping a network journal during your search. In it, you can record all of your contacts and networking activities, as well as comments on what worked and what didn't. Next time you need to network, you can use your journal as a guide instead of starting at square one.

PART·THREE

INFORMATIONAL
INTERVIEWING:

THE ULTIMATE NETWORKING TECHNIQUE

Chapter Sixteen

WHAT IS INFORMATIONAL INTERVIEWING?

Here's a startling statistic: One out of every two hundred resumes (some studies put the number as high as fifteen hundred resumes) results in a job offer. One out of every twelve informational interviews, however, results in a job offer. That's why informational interviewing is the ultimate networking technique, especially considering that the purpose of informational interviewing is to gather information, not solicit job offers. Job offers just happen to be a delightful side benefit of this valuable practice.

Informational interviewing is just what it sounds like—interviewing designed to produce information. What kind of information? The information you need to choose or refine a career path, learn how to break in, and find out if you have what it takes to succeed. Informational interviewing is an expanded form of chatting with your network contacts. It's the process of engaging one of your network contacts in a highly focused conversation that provides you with key information you need to launch or boost your career. The term "informational interviewing" was invented by Richard Nelson Bolles, author of the best-selling career guide of all time, *What Color Is Your Parachute?* Bolles refers to the process as "trying on jobs to see if they fit you." He notes that most people screen jobs and companies after they've already taken a job, while informational interviewing gives you the opportunity to conduct the screening process before going after or accepting a position.

An informational interview is not the same as a job interview by any means, but it is probably the most effective form of networking there is. I require my students to perform three informational interviews per semester. Most of them are skeptical about the assignment in the beginning, but I can't tell you how many have ended the semester amazed and delighted with how much they learned and how influential the process was for their careers. I'm not the only teacher whose students have been thrilled with informational interviews. Terry Carles, a student recruitment counselor at Valencia Community College reports, "I teach career development, and my students are required to do an informational interview. Every semester, someone returns with a job, internship, etc., from their experience. One student completed an informational interview with a network administrator, and returned the next week with a $23,000-a-year job offer."

I've had students who have realized as a result of informational interviewing that their career paths and even their majors were totally wrong for them. They made this discovery when there was still time to make a course correction. Others haven't needed such a drastic change but have adjusted their assumptions and expectations based on what they learned in the interviews. When you are considering entering or changing to a certain career, it just makes all kinds of sense to talk to people in that field. Yet most people never do. They trust their professors, textbooks, or romantic notions about professions gleaned from TV or movies. When you really think about it, you miss out on an incredible opportunity if you fail to research your career field by talking to people in it.

FOOT  NOTE

Although informational interviewing is well known and highly promoted in the world of career counselors, it is an underused—and often even unfamiliar—practice among job seekers. My students have repeatedly demonstrated the value of informational interviewing, especially as a self-discovery tool. As one student wrote, "The informational interview process was extremely eye-opening. I went from a clueless college student to a directed job seeker. Before this experience, I was unaware of how helpful talking with professionals can be. I was able to ascertain what these jobs really entailed. I got a feel for what the working world is all about. My conversations with my interviewers gave me a window into how to get into the job I want. I learned from people who are living my dream now that I need to prepare for the future."

THE BEST WAY TO LEARN WHAT YOU REALLY WANT IN A CAREER

Because of the exploratory nature of informational interviews, they are particularly effective for those, such as college students, who are just embarking on their careers. They are also an excellent tool for career changers who want to find out what's involved in the career they are considering entering. Even for those who don't wish to change careers but do want to change jobs, informational interviews can be a helpful way of discovering what working for other companies would be like. A job seeker who does an informational interview usually has his career path illuminated in one of the following ways:

- The inexperienced job seeker learns about the realities of the work world and what to expect.

- The job seeker learns what types of opportunities are available in a given field, including jobs and career paths she may not have known existed.

- The job seeker's career aspiration is affirmed. The dream career turns out to be everything he thought it would be.

- The job seeker's career path is reinforced, but she learns that more training or more polished skills will be necessary for success in the field. Or

FOOT NOTE

My students have found that informational interviewing arms them with the wisdom to make better decisions, as this student describes: "Informational interviews gave me an opportunity to explore the knowledge, advice, and experience of successful professionals. They helped educate me about current employment conditions, the future of the field, and the many other aspects essential in choosing a career direction. Following the interviews, I found I was better equipped to make decisions about my future and definitely more comfortable in making those decisions."

COLLEGE STUDENT CHARTS CAREER PATH AFTER SEVEN YEARS ADRIFT

"I walked away from informational interviewing with something more valuable than an internship, a job, or even a foot in the door at my interviewee's place of employment. I walked away with the information I needed to formulate a career path for my future. Ever since I was a freshman in high school, I would put myself into a deep depression by pondering what I was going to do with my life. I did not have a clue as to what I could do to make myself happy and earn a decent living. My family and friends calmed me by pointing out that I was only a freshman, and there was plenty of time to find my career path. Little did they know that six years later, as a junior in college, I would be deliberating [on] this same issue. It is for this reason that I used informational interviews, not for a job, but for information to help me choose my path. In searching for a career, I have performed many assessment tests, read profiles of jobs in career service centers, and researched various companies on the Internet, none of which provided me with the insight of an actual worker in the field, or an entrepreneur who made his way. I learned a great deal about the skills needed to be successful in the business world as well as in life from informational interviews. Most importantly, after seven years of deliberation, the verdict is in as to what my future holds for me."

the job seeker learns of his or her professional strengths and weaknesses and often receives a resume critique. The job seeker sometimes has an opportunity to promote her strengths in a nonthreatening environment.

• The career the job seeker always wanted turns out to be wrong for him. I had a student who began the semester 100 percent sure he wanted to be a stockbroker. After interviewing three stockbrokers, he ended the semester 100 percent sure he did not want to be a stockbroker. Many job seekers learn through informational interviews that the career's average salary, working conditions, or opportunities for advancement are not what they imagined. Or they learn that the career just doesn't fit their personality.

• A job seeker who interviews people in several different careers obtains the information needed to choose from among various career paths. Or the job seeker who is set on a general path to pursue narrows down a specific niche through informational interviewing. A new graduate who wants to get into marketing, for example, may decide as the result of informational interviews whether to pursue marketing research, sales, or promotions.

• A job seeker who conducts informational interviews with several companies discovers an excellent fit within an organization and decides that it would be a wonderful company to work for.

FOOT  NOTE

Informational interviewing makes the work world real to those who haven't yet experienced it, as one of my students notes: "It wasn't until I conducted informational interviews that I began to assess my career objectives for the first time—thinking about the environment I would like to work in, the types of people I want to work with, and the schedule I would have. It is because of the interviews that my career objectives have changed somewhat, and I have come to realize exactly what I would like to receive and give back to my future job."

- The job seeker gleans the information needed to develop a strategy for entering his or her career of choice.

- The job seeker clarifies values, realizing what's really important in life and choosing a career that allows him or her to embrace what's important.

YOU CAN BENEFIT FROM INFORMATIONAL INTERVIEWING AT VIRTUALLY ANY STAGE OF YOUR CAREER:

- The early stage, when you are exploring which career path to pursue

- The middle stage, when you are finalizing career choices and deciding on a niche within your career path

- The late stage, when you are deciding which companies to apply to and preparing to interview for jobs

- The stages revisited, when you are ready to change careers and begin the cycle anew

- The stage in which you don't want to change careers, but you'd like to explore other companies to see if the grass is really greener

A WAY TO TAP INTO THE HIDDEN JOB MARKET

Informational interviewing is one of the best ways to mine the hidden job market because of the depth and quality of information the practice provides. Those who conduct informational interviews can learn

- The needs of the company or department that is the subject of the interview. Armed with this knowledge, the job seeker can later approach the company with a description of how she can meet these needs (see Part 4).

- Valuable insider knowledge about how to break into and succeed in the chosen career and company. Consider a future job interview in which your competition is someone who has conducted an informational interview with a company employee, and you haven't. Which one of you do you think will have the edge in the job interview?

• The names of the other companies that may be hiring

• The names of other contacts who can become part of the job seeker's network

• Timely information about industry trends and issues, which can provide an inside edge in the job search

• How to "speak the language"—the jargon of the industry

• Unadvertised job openings within the company. Sometimes the unadvertised opening is the very one your informational interviewee holds! Tammy Bowen, a director of career planning, tells of conducting an informational interview when she was relocating to a new area. The woman she interviewed had just accepted another position elsewhere and called Bowen to ask if she would be interested in taking her job. Bowen was then invited for a job interview and subsequently was offered the job, which she accepted. The same thing happened to Jerry Falco, director of the Career Development Center at Lycoming College. "I got my first job after college in a matter of days through networking," Falco recalls. "My girlfriend's sister was dating a pharmaceutical salesman. I called [him] for an informational interview. The salesman gave me the

FOOT NOTE

Informational interviewing is a great way to get your networking feet wet, as one of my students learned: "The informational interview experience taught me a lot about myself, the importance of communication skills, future contacts, and how the interview process works. Throughout the interview process, I wasn't certain about my future direction, but as the interview process evolved, so did I."

district manager's name and number. The salesman had just announced his plan to continue his education full-time, and a replacement was needed. I did not know this when I called. I called the district manager and arranged a meeting for the next morning. I was offered the job less than a week later."

INFORMATIONAL INTERVIEWING TO BUILD NETWORKING RELATIONSHIPS

At the very least, you can count each informational interviewee as a valuable member of your network of contacts. Because your conversation with an informational interviewee will tend to go into greater depth than your chats with other members of your network, you will generally forge a stronger and more memorable bond. Informational interviewing builds relationships with people who become invested in your career, will remember you, and will be eager to hear about your progress.

People in the world of work are generally delighted to give informational interviews for the same reasons they are willing to be included as a member of your network. They like to talk about themselves and give advice. They are often especially eager to do their part to recruit a new member of their profession and encourage those just starting out in the field. Information and advice are easy to give, as opposed to actually trying to put people into jobs.

PRACTICE THAT YOU CAN APPLY TO JOB INTERVIEWS

An informational interview is not the same as a job interview. Essentially, you are in control of an informational interview; you set the agenda; you ask the questions. Despite the differences, however, informational interviewing gives you valuable practice in talking with people one-on-one in a professional setting. Because the atmosphere of the informational interview is relatively relaxed compared to that of a job interview, you can use these situations to bolster your confidence so that you are exuding self-assurance when you interview for an actual job opening. The more informational interviews you conduct, the more confident you will be. My students have also discovered that informational interviewing helps them practice their communication skills, their listening skills, and their ability to interact with many types of people. Wrote one of my students, a senior finance major: "Informational interviewing has helped me to realize how important communication skills are in pursuing success. Before the interviews, I was never a person who would approach someone much older than me and strike up a conversation. After conducting the interviews, though, I have much more confidence in myself and know that if I wanted to have a conversation with someone more experienced than me, I could."

WHAT IT'S NOT:
A SNEAKY WAY TO INTERVIEW FOR A JOB

The practice of informational interviewing is not without its abusers. Too many job seekers have arranged interviews on the pretext that they are informational but then have tried to turn the sessions into job interviews. So much abuse has occurred, in fact, that some employers are extremely wary of being interviewed, while others have been burned and refuse to be fooled again. If you've had any thoughts of trying to be dishonest about your motives for informational interviewing, put this book down and hang your head in shame. Ask yourself if you would hire someone who had deceived you about the purpose of his or her interview with you. And trust me when I tell you that informational interviewing is phenomenally effective without any deceit. Job and internship offers often result from informational interviews, but getting offers should not be the purpose of the interviews. Remember that the information and insight you gain from this process is exceedingly valuable in its own right.

INFORMATIONAL INTERVIEWING GIVES HER THE CONFIDENCE TO CHANGE HER LIFE

"I did not want to do informational interviews because I am rather shy. I knew that it would be so hard for me to call up people and ask them questions. I actually feared it. I turned to my parents to ask for their help. Luckily they had a multitude of friends and business associates I could interview. My first interviewee quickly started to change my mind [about informational interviewing]. This interviewee obtained her job through an informational interview. When I learned this fact, I started to take notice of how beneficial these interviews could be if I utilized them. I found myself having shorter versions of informational interviews with a variety of people. At work, I would ask the district manager how he started out, or when the vice president came to the store, I would ask him a few questions. I realized that if I had never done the interviews, I would have been too scared and insecure to go over and talk to someone I did not know.

"Finally I was starting to realize what informational interviews were about and how I could use them in my career. I began to think about all the people I had talked to, and I began to look at my future very differently. I always thought that I would finish college, go on to law school, graduate, and get a job as a lawyer for a big corporation. I had never questioned that path. I thought it was the only logical way. This misconception was changed after these interviews. I began to think that there were so many different things I could do, things I had never even imagined. I spent a great deal of time thinking about my future and exactly how I wanted to live it. I began thinking about the variety of careers in a different light. I was not distinguishing them by how much they paid or the status I would receive from them anymore. I was now looking at them and all the different aspects about them. I began considering the number of hours I would have to work, if I would have to relocate, and if it would allow me to obtain my other goals as well.

"The informational interviews taught me one other lesson that has had the biggest impact on my future—all the options I had. It is an amazing experience the first time that you realize you're no longer a child and that you are really going to enter the real world soon. I am not inexperienced; I supported myself through college by working full-time as a waitress. I always thought I would wait tables till I graduated from law school. I remember the day my opinion changed, and so did my future. I was no longer happy with my job; actually, I was miserable. I found myself sitting there listening to the manager of my restaurant complain about things going wrong, all of which were very obviously her fault. I began to ask her a couple of questions, the same questions that I had asked my informational interviewees. I discovered that this woman had not been to college, held no degree, and she had been promoted on a fluke. I sat there thinking that this woman is in way over her head and that she has no idea about what it takes to run this restaurant. I thought of all the simple lessons and ideas that I had learned in school and how they could reform this restaurant immediately.

"That was it! I could do this. I could manage a restaurant. I had finally realized that I had a great education and four years of experience working for me. I spoke to my parents and really believed that I was going to let them in on this big secret. I was wrong. I was met with a response that shocked me, 'Of course you can do it.'

"All of a sudden I looked at myself differently. I was not only an adult, I was an adult with an education that has given me a field of choices. So I did it. I grabbed the newspaper and began looking for jobs. I found [an ad for] one and decided to give it a try. I rewrote my resume, and sent it out. Four days later I received a call from the company to set up an interview. I was on my way. I have begun to plan my life out differently, investigating what I could do with the degrees I have now—not waiting until law school is over.

"These informational interviews taught me so many things. I now realize I have so many wonderful things I can do with my life, not three years from now, but now. I never thought that I would say that I was happy to do informational interviews, but now I can say that this one activity changed my life for the better."

Chapter Seventeen

HOW TO FIND AND CHOOSE INTERVIEWEES: NETWORK, NETWORK, NETWORK

The easiest way to find prospective informational interviewees is through networking. Anyone in your network either can be the subject of an informational interview or can suggest others to interview. The ideal subject of an informational interview is someone who is in a job you'd like to have, either in the near future or someday. The interviewees in higher-level jobs you'd like to hold someday can be advantageous because they may also possess hiring power. Naturally, if you interview someone with hiring power, you increase your chances of receiving a job offer as a direct result of the informational interview. But remember that obtaining offers is not the purpose of these interviews. It's fine to interview people with hiring power, but you will likely learn more from people at your own level (and, depending on your level, your peers may have hiring power anyway). Favor information over influence, but aim for a mix of interviewees with and without hiring power.

Even if you are still unsure of what you want to do in your career, you may find that informational interviews are helpful in narrowing down your list of career choices. Chances are that you are considering a few careers at the top of your list—choose the top three and line up interviews with people in those fields. The process of interviewing may help you decide what path you want to follow.

Scrutinize your network for people who would make good informational interview subjects. Among the best sources for informational interviews for college students and new grads are alumni, especially recent alumni who are in the kind of job you expect to occupy right out of college. Company representatives who recruit on your campus are also good targets for informational interviews. They are frequently asked to perform this function, and they are also usually quite adept in providing information on working for their company.

The best sources for informational interviews for established job seekers and career changers include members of professional organizations. If no one in your network fits that description, start asking members of your network to suggest people who hold the type of job you'd like.

Don't be afraid to shoot for pie-in-the-sky interviewees. If you'd love to interview Michael Eisner or Bill Gates, but not surprisingly, no one in your network knows one of these superstars, try approaching them cold. Granted, success is pretty unlikely, but it can't hurt to ask, and some very powerful titans of business have actually granted informational interviews on occasion.

Once you've identified some people to interview, you can approach them using the suggestions in Chapter 18.

How many interviews should you conduct? As a matter of fact, informational interviewing can be a rich and fulfilling lifelong process. You could spend your whole career learning about other people's jobs while enjoying your own. You can also spend a lot of time on informational interviewing in the early formative years of your career when you're still exploring what you'd like to do. It's wise to interview several people in any one type of job to get a variety of perspectives. You wouldn't want to base your whole opinion about a given job on an interview with someone who was burned out on the position or carrying a chip on his shoulder.

The number of interviews you conduct at any given time when you are searching for a job will depend a great deal on the urgency of your job hunt. On one hand, informational interviews are time consuming, both to arrange and conduct. On the other hand, they are highly effective. If your job search is urgent, employ other networking techniques and conventional job-search methods, but always keep at least a few informational interviews in the mix. I assign my students, generally college juniors, to do three informational interviews as part of my class. If I could, I would probably assign at least ten. You will be your own best judge of how many will benefit you and your career.

Chapter Eighteen

HOW TO SET UP INFORMATIONAL INTERVIEWS

Before you even approach your prospective interviewees, you need to think about what you are actually requesting.

DECIDING ON A FRAMEWORK: IN PERSON, BY PHONE, OR VIA E-MAIL?

Should you ask to conduct the interview over the phone, through e-mail, or in person? Face-to-face interviews are by far the most valuable and effective. To talk to someone in his or her own workplace environment can be so much more instructive than talking over the phone or on-line. You can observe so much more of the corporate culture during an in-person interview. You are also much more likely to make a lasting and productive connection with your interviewee and more likely to receive a job offer.

Face-to-face interviews are not always possible, however. Sometimes geography is the obstacle; someone you'd really like to interview is just too far away to make a visit practical. Time constraints also may play a

FOOT  NOTE

As with any networking, making that first contact can feel like a major obstacle, especially if you're shy. Once you do it, as one of my students learned, it gets a lot easier: "I learned quite a bit about myself while doing these interviews. Some of my biggest faults have shown up . . . including overwhelming shyness. I had to learn to be assertive . . . to call up complete strangers and ask for interviews. I became more outspoken and confident."

role. Even though a phone or e-mail interview can be just as time consuming as a face-to-face meeting, prospective interviewees sometimes perceive in-person interviews as more of a disruption than those conducted via other means.

Ultimately, the framework should be the interviewee's decision, but when you initially approach the subject to request an interview, it's a good idea to express your preference.

HOW MUCH TIME SHOULD YOU ASK FOR?

The rule of thumb for informational interviews is to ask for twenty to thirty minutes. Once you're in the interview, it's important to stick to that limit unless you get clear signals from the interviewee that he or she would like the meeting to continue for a longer period.

USING REFERRALS TO HELP SET UP INFORMATIONAL INTERVIEWS

People in your network can be invaluable to you in setting up informational interviews. They can help in two ways.

They can directly run interference for you by contacting someone you'd like to interview. Let's say your Uncle Ed knows a head honcho at a company you'd love to work for. Uncle Ed calls Mr. Big, and after the appropriate small talk, says, "My nephew, Charlie, is looking for a job in your field and would love to conduct an informational interview with you to find out more about your career. Do you mind if he contacts you to arrange an appointment?" Mr. Big responds, "No problem. I'd love to help out. I look forward to hearing from Charlie."

Members of your network can also assist you by simply allowing you to use their names as a referral. In that case, perhaps Uncle Ed hasn't gone so far as to pave the way for you but says it's fine to use his name. Thus, when you contact Mr. Big, you can say, "My uncle, Ed Matthews, suggested I contact you to see if you might be able to meet with me for thirty minutes to tell me about your career."

WHAT TO INCLUDE IN YOUR REQUEST
FOR AN INTERVIEW

Whether you initially write, call, or e-mail, your request should:

• Identify you

• Explain why you're contacting this person

• Tell how you got the person's name, if applicable

• Assure the prospective interviewee that you need only a brief meeting

• Assure her that you are not looking for a job in this interview (if these concerns arise)

• Offer in-person, phone, or e-mail choices for conducting the interview

• Express appreciation to the prospective interviewee for considering the interview.

WRITING LETTERS OR SENDING E-MAILS
TO REQUEST INFORMATIONAL INTERVIEWS

Unless you are extremely adept at using the phone and rejection rolls right off your back, you will probably find it much easier to write a letter or send an e-mail message first, and then follow up with a phone call. The following sample letters are easily adaptable as e-mail requests. Be sure to keep copies of all your correspondence.

LETTER FROM A COLLEGE STUDENT

Dear Dr. Buddinger:

As a junior at Franklin and Marshall College, I have begun taking classes in my major field of psychology. I am especially interested in the pediatric therapy track, and I would like the opportunity to schedule an informational interview with you to learn more about the day-to-day activities of a pediatric therapist.

I was fascinated with the approach to pediatric therapy that you described in your recent article in *Pediatric Therapy Today*, and I feel you would be one of the most enlightening people in the field that I could possibly interview.

I know you are very busy, so I assure you our meeting will be brief. It would be wonderful for me to meet with you face-to-face and see your clinic, but I am also open to interviewing by phone or e-mail. I'd like to give you a call next week to schedule about a half hour of your time, at your convenience.

Thank you so much for considering this request.

Cordially,

Pippa Carson

LETTER FROM A CAREER CHANGER BASED ON A REFERRAL

Dear Mr. Skaarsgard:

I am a high school art teacher seriously contemplating a career change to the art conservation field. Regina Twigg told me about your wonderful gallery and suggested that you could offer a unique perspective on this career field.

I would appreciate the opportunity to meet with you and discuss your work and the trends in the field. I am especially interested in your views regarding conservation and restoration of Native American artwork. Any insights you have would be greatly appreciated.

I do not intend to take more than about thirty minutes of your time. I would be pleased to meet you in person and view your gallery; however, I would also be willing to interview you by phone or e-mail.

I will contact your office the week of September 17 to see if we can set up a mutually convenient time for this informational meeting.

Thank you very much for your consideration.

Sincerely,

Ted Thistlebine

LETTER BASED ON PREVIOUS ENCOUNTER

Dear Ms. Milton:

I really enjoyed meeting you after your presentation at the last meeting of the Brandon County Human Resources Association. Your talk was truly inspiring.

I am currently a personnel generalist looking to expand my horizons within the human resources field and would welcome the opportunity to hear more of your insights into the profession. Your position sounds very much like the type of work I'd like to do.

Would you have time in the next few weeks to meet with me for about a half hour? I'd like to ask you a few questions about your role in this profession. I would be happy to come to your office to talk, but if it would be more convenient, we could conduct the interview by phone or e-mail.

Thank you so much for considering this request. I'll contact you next week to see if we can schedule a time to meet.

Cordially,

Pamela Hotchkiss

CAREER CHANGER'S COLD-CONTACT LETTER

Dear Mr. Pondo:

As an aspiring management consultant, I have been impressed with what I've learned about Davie and Associates. Your company's reputation for high-quality work has inspired me to request a brief informational interview with you. I was especially interested to read in the *Wall Street Journal* about your company's new twist on total quality management.

I am completing graduate work in management consulting at Bowdoin College after leaving active military service. I would very much like to talk with you about your work.

Because of the obvious geographical obstacles, an in-person meeting is not practical, so I'd like to interview you by phone or e-mail.

I'll contact you the week of November 19 to see if we can set up a time for a phone or e-mail discussion. I will ensure that the interview does not take more than thirty minutes of your valuable time.

Thanks so much for considering this request.

Cordially,

Dan Deerfield

PHONING TO REQUEST AN INFORMATIONAL INTERVIEW

Your initial request can be by telephone if you are comfortable with speaking to people on the phone. Or perhaps you are on a tight time frame and don't have time to introduce yourself by letter or e-mail. Although it is possible to set up an entire informational interview via e-mail, you will almost definitely have to call your interviewee sooner or later if you've written or e-mailed first. Never expect the interviewee to contact you.

If your initial contact is by phone, it's extremely helpful to have been referred to your prospective interviewee by a mutual acquaintance. It's also helpful if you're a student since working people often especially enjoy helping students. Whatever your situation, your call will most likely be intercepted by a gatekeeper—a receptionist, secretary, or assistant. These people need not be thought of as obstacles, and a little courtesy and respect should enable you to connect with the person you want to interview. Let's look at a possible scenario:

> *Secretary answering interviewee's phone:* Bill Jones's office; Nancy Fredericks speaking.
>
> *You:* Good morning, Nancy (or Ms. Fredericks). How are you today? My name is _____. May I speak to Mr. Jones?
>
> *Nancy:* Will he know what this is in reference to?
>
> *You, if you've written a letter first:* I'm following up on a letter I sent him last week.
>
> OR *(a bit more boldly):* He's expecting my call. (If you said in your letter that you would call, this statement is perfectly true.)
>
> OR *(if you've been referred to Mr. Jones by someone else):* Stu Ross suggested I call Mr. Jones.
>
> OR *(if you're a student):* I'm a student at _____ [name of university], and I wanted to see if I could schedule a very brief meeting with Mr. Jones to find out more about his career.

Any of those responses on your part should get you past the gatekeeper. Experts suggest that, in business, Tuesdays, Wednesdays, and Thursdays are less busy than Mondays or Fridays and you will be more likely to be put through on those days. Often the gatekeeper will be willing to put you through, but it's impossible to do so because your prospective interviewee is out of the office, in a meeting, or on another line. If you are asked if you'd like to leave a message, it's best to inquire about a good time to call back. Since you want to avoid leaving the interviewee with any obligation to call you back, it's better to try to phone him again later. If you've tried repeatedly to call back and never find the interviewee in, you could leave a message asking that he call back, but don't hold your breath.

Many experts advise that if you've tried unsuccessfully a number of times to reach your target, it's okay to employ some techniques for avoiding the gatekeeper altogether. Leaving a voice mail message is more effective than leaving a message with a gatekeeper who is not getting you through the gate. The kinds of people you want to interview often come to work early and stay late. Try calling early in the morning, and you may find your interviewee answering her own phone. Or you may be connected to the interviewee's voice mail. If so, however, remember that the voice mail is just another avenue for paving the way. You don't want to leave the impression that you expect the interviewee to call *you* back. Always keep the ball in your own court. A pave-the-way voice mail message might be

> Hello, Mr. Jones. This is Kitty Farr calling. I am exploring possible career directions and am interested in interviewing you very briefly about your career. I'll call you back on Wednesday morning to talk to you personally about scheduling a short meeting.

Possible alternatives based on your situation:

> Hello, Mr. Jones. This is Kitty Farr calling. I'm following up on my letter (or e-mail) of last week requesting to interview you very briefly about your career. I'll call you back on Wednesday morning to talk to you personally about scheduling a short meeting.

> Hello, Mr. Jones. This is Kitty Farr calling. Stu Ross suggested I contact you about interviewing you very briefly regarding your career. I'll call you back on Wednesday morning to talk to you personally about scheduling a short meeting.

> Hello, Mr. Jones. This is Kitty Farr calling. I'm a student at Albright University, and I'm interested in interviewing you very briefly about your career. I'll call you back on Wednesday morning to talk to you personally about scheduling a short meeting.

SAMPLE PHONE SCRIPTS FOR DIRECT DIALOGUE WITH INTERVIEWEE

Once you are talking with the actual person you want to interview, here are some suggested scripts. Of course, you don't want to sound as though you're reading from a script, but these samples will give you an idea of what to say. Always ask if it is a good time to talk. If the prospective interviewee indicates that you haven't called at a good time, ask if there is a better time to call back.

For a cold call:

Hi, my name is _____. Do you have a few moments? [Wait for response.] I'm in the process of making some career decisions and have discovered through my research that your company is doing some exciting things. I would like to see if I could schedule an appointment to conduct a short interview with you about your career. I would not take any more than thirty minutes of your time.

For a referral:

Hi, my name is _____. Karen Levy suggested I contact you. Have I caught you at a good time? [Wait for response.] Karen tells me you'd be a great person to talk to about a career in _____. I'm exploring that field and wondered if we might be able to have a short meeting so I could ask you some questions about your career and get your perspective on the field.

For a self-referral based on seeing the prospective interviewee speak:

Hi, my name is _____. I was at the meeting of the American Marketing Association last week and really enjoyed the talk you gave. Do you have a few minutes? [Wait for response.] I'm interested in breaking into marketing and would love to schedule a brief meeting to get your advice. When I heard you speak, I knew it would be enlightening to talk with you about your marketing career. I need only about thirty minutes of your time.

For a self-referral based on a previous encounter:

Hi, this is _____. I really enjoyed meeting you at Zach Howell's party last Saturday. Our brief chat affirmed my interest in investment banking. Are you terribly busy right now? [Wait for response.] It was great to chat with you, and I wondered if you might have a half hour in which we could continue our conversation sometime soon.

For a student:

Hi, my name is _____. I'm a student at Kensington University majoring in _____, and I'm plotting out my career path. Is this a good time for you? [Wait for response.] Would it be possible for me to conduct a short interview with you so I can get your advice and find out more about your job? I promise I wouldn't take more than half an hour of your time.

For a letter or e-mail follow-up:

Hi, my name is _____. I wrote you a letter last week. Is this a good time to talk? [Wait for response.] As you recall, I am interested in the _____ field, and I wrote to ask if you could spare thirty minutes to talk with me about your career. Do you think we could schedule a meeting?

For a voice mail follow-up:

Hi, my name is _____. I left you a voice-mail message yesterday. Did I catch you at a good time? [Wait for response.] As you recall, I was calling to see if I could arrange to interview you briefly about your career.

As the prospective interviewee agrees and begins to suggest times, don't put roadblocks in the way. Do whatever you must to accommodate the interviewee's schedule. The interviewee is doing you a big favor, so it's your responsibility to be flexible.

ASKING IN PERSON FOR AN INFORMATIONAL INTERVIEW

There's always the possibility you'll meet someone face-to-face who would make a fabulous informational interview subject. If it's a chance meeting, you might spontaneously mention that you'd love to interview the person. You will probably still have to follow up by phone or e-mail to arrange the actual appointment.

HANDLING RESISTANCE TO INFORMATIONAL INTERVIEWS

As noted earlier, informational interviews have been abused to the degree that some employers are wary of or downright opposed to them. If a prospective interviewee seems hesitant about your request, don't push too hard. If you sense a crack in his or her resistance, you can simply assure the person that you seek only information; you are not trying to sneak your way into a job interview. If you are student, be sure to mention that fact since many employers are more willing to assist students than other job seekers. But if the prospective interviewee seems too uncomfortable with the idea, cut your losses and move on to the next person.

Another type of resistance can come from the prospective interviewee who suggests that you should be talking to the company personnel director or human resources manager. In that case, tell the would-be interviewee that you are not seeking the interview to actively pursue a job; instead, at this stage, you are merely seeking information that will help you make some career decisions.

You might also be told the company has no openings. Again, explain that you are not pursuing openings but simply information; you will not be in a position to seek job openings until you have gathered more information about the field.

Some people might be ostensibly willing to be interviewed but tell you they are too busy. Don't press them, but do ask if they anticipate a time when they might have a few minutes for an interview. Or ask if they know someone else in a similar position who might have time to meet with you—which is also a terrific way to expand your network.

Informational Interviewing

Chapter Nineteen

HOW TO PREPARE FOR
AN INFORMATIONAL INTERVIEW

For an informational interview to be truly effective, you can't just go into it blindly. You need to prepare.

RESEARCH THE COMPANY

Thorough company research is an absolute necessity when you go on a regular job interview. You don't have to do quite as much research for an informational interview, but some degree of research will enhance the quality of the interview. If you are informed about the company, you'll be able to ask more intelligent and relevant questions. You'll respond thoughtfully to information and questions the interviewee might put to you. You won't waste the person's time by asking questions that could have been answered by doing your homework. A wealth of valuable resources are available for company research, many of them right at your fingertips on the Internet. Two excellent umbrella Web sites that walk you through the whole process of company research are the Quintessential Careers Researching Companies site at *http://www.quintcareers.com/researching_companies.html* and Researching Companies on the Internet—A Tutorial at *http://home.sprintmail.com/~debflanagan/*. Other resources include:

- **Library reference material.** Check with your reference librarian on how to find company information. Some standard reference sources, both about companies and occupations in general, include *The Occupational Outlook Handbook, The Dictionary of Occupational Titles, U.S. Industrial Outlook,* and *The 100 Best Companies to Work for in America.*

- **Library on-line and CD-ROM databases.** Examples include Lexis/ Nexis, ABI/INFORM, EbscoHost Business, NewsBank InfoWeb, Reference USA Business, and Business and Industry News. These databases direct you to articles about companies found in recent periodicals. The database will either direct you to the periodical that contains the article or will actually contain the article in full-text form, accessible right from the database.

- **Annual reports.** You can request them from the company itself. A selection of annual reports also may be available in your library. Many annual reports can also be viewed on the World Wide Web. More than one thousand can be accessed through *http://www.reportgallery.com/*. You can order annual reports through the *Public Register*'s free annual report service at *http://www.prars.com/*. Many companies also have annual reports for the current and recent past years in the investor relations section of their Web sites.

- **Other company literature.** Contact the company to ask for any brochures, newsletters, or other publications that would familiarize you with the organization.

- **Company Web pages.** If you don't know a company's Web address, you can try two easy steps. Try typing in *www.companyname.com*, where "companyname" is the actual name of the firm. Or conduct a search on one or more of the Web's many search engines, such as GoTo.com, Lycos, Excite, or Yahoo. Another option, of course, is to call the company and ask for the Web site address.

- **University career services offices.** These offices contain lots of company information for college students, and generally alumni may use the resources of their university's career center as well.

It's also a good idea whenever possible to find out as much as you can about the person you'll be interviewing. If you were referred to your interviewee by someone, ask that person to tell you about the individual you'll be interviewing.

DECIDE WHETHER AND HOW YOU WILL
RECORD INFORMATION

Consider whether you'd like to document any of what you learn during the interview, and if so, how. You may find it especially helpful to have a record of the interviews if you do a lot of them and want to keep track of which interview yielded which information. Notes can be a valuable resource when, as you switch into full job-hunting mode, you go back and contact the companies you especially liked. When you encounter an employer you'd really like to work for, take notes about the company's needs so you can later use your ability to meet these needs as a selling point when applying for a job there (see Chapter 25). You'll also definitely want to jot down the names of any additional contacts your interviewees refer you to. Options for recording information include

- **Taking notes on a small notepad.** Try to be unobtrusive, and don't be writing furiously every moment of the interview. You want to give your interviewee your full attention, so jot down only the most important information.

- **Tape recording.** The most important thing about tape recording is to obtain your interviewee's permission before you record. Use a tape recorder that is small and easy to use so that it won't disrupt the interview. Also realize that transcribing a taped interview is a time-consuming process.

- **Trusting your memory.** Going into the interview without any way to record what you learn is an option, but you may want to plant a notepad in your purse or car, so you can quickly write down everything you remember right afterward. You will, if course, need to have some way to take down the names and numbers of any referrals you receive.

PLAN TO DRESS FOR SUCCESS

For maximum effectiveness, dress in professional attire for an informational interview—the same way you would for a job interview. Men should wear a full suit with tie; women should ideally wear a skirted suit or very professional pantsuit. Your clothing should be clean and pressed with no rips or tears, and your shoes shined. Wear conservative jewelry and go easy on the fragrance. Be sure hair and fingernails are nicely groomed. Hair should be worn off your face. The interview is a chance to make a positive impression. Not everyone who is gathering information will go to such lengths to look professional. You will distinguish yourself if you look as though you fit in with the organization. Obviously, none of this advice applies to telephone or e-mail interviews, but even when you use those communication channels, you'll project yourself more confidently if you wear something nicer than, say, your ratty old bathrobe.

UPDATE AND BRING YOUR RESUME

Let us once again stress that the informational interview is not a job interview. Still make sure your resume is updated and bring a copy with you. For one thing, your interviewee may well ask for a copy. "As someone who has spent ten years in human resources, I'd have to say that if I were meeting with someone for an informational interview and they did not have a resume, I'd think that they were unprepared and therefore maybe not such a top candidate for a future opening," cautions Robbin Beauchamp, employer relations coordinator at Stonehill College. "Any job seeker, regardless of age or experience, should be able to easily get their hands on their most current, updated resume. Keep them in the car!"

If you are not asked for your resume, consider asking the interviewee to take a look at your resume at the end of the interview. Ask whether she could offer any suggestions for making the resume a more effective tool for obtaining a job in her field or company. Keep in mind that request for a quick resume critique will be met much more receptively if you've established excellent rapport with the interviewee. The ability to leave your resume or ask for a resume critique is one clear advantage of conducting face-to-face interviews.

"I tell students to go prepared with their resumes but that they might not get a chance to use them," notes Bill Fletcher, director of career and experiential education at the College of Mount St. Joseph. There's always a chance an employer may ask for one to find out more about the student and to decide which areas to cover in the interview.

Informational Interviewing

Since some employers like to prepare as much as possible for the interview, you may be asked to send your resume before the interview. Even if you're not asked to, it may be a good idea. After your initial phone or e-mail conversation with the interviewee, decide whether he would benefit from or respond well to receiving your resume beforehand, and if so, send it on.

If you receive advice during the interview for better tailoring your resume to that industry, consider asking—again, only if your rapport with the interviewee has been exceptional—if you can send the resume to the interviewee after making changes and call him for an opinion on the new version.

Having said all this, however, you may occasionally encounter advice telling you not to take your resume to an informational interview. One reasonable justification is that only after the informational interview will you be able to tailor your resume specifically to the kind of job you learned about. "I recommend not taking a resume to an informational interview," says Elaine Balych of Mount Royal College in Canada. "All the information learned in the informational interview is fodder for tailoring your resume to reflect the needs of that employer. If that employer gets your old resume—without the information learned—the job hunter is not positioning himself or herself strategically. What I recommend is that the job hunter be prepared to deal with the request in a very fast turnaround such as 'I do not have one with me at this time but would be happy to put one in your hands in the next twenty-four or forty-eight hours.'"

PRACTICE WITH A FRIEND OR FAMILY MEMBER

If you haven't done much interviewing, ease yourself in by interviewing close friends or family members before you conduct an informational interview with someone you don't know well. There's probably a lot you don't know about the jobs of those close to you, so in addition to obtaining valuable practice, you may even learn something.

CALL TO CONFIRM YOUR APPOINTMENT

The day before your interview, call to confirm that the meeting is still on. Confirm also the interview time, and make sure you know how to get to the interview site.

PREPARE A LIST OF QUESTIONS

Sometimes in informational interviews you'll find that conversation flows very naturally and spontaneously. In most cases, however, you will need to steer the interview in the direction most helpful to you by asking questions. For a thirty-minute interview, a list of fifteen questions should be plenty, but you should be prepared with a few extras in case your interviewee gives very concise responses or wants you to stay longer. The list of two hundred questions in the next chapter would probably be enough to last for days, so how do you narrow down the list? Most important is to ask the questions you most want answered. And you are certainly not limited to the questions in this book.

Keep yes-or-no questions to a minimum. Open-ended questions are far more effective because the interviewee will have to elaborate on the answers instead of responding in monosyllables.

Finally, prioritize your questions: If you don't have enough time to ask them all, at least you will have asked the ones that are most important to you. Focus on questions whose answers cannot easily be found elsewhere, such as in the company literature.

 FOOT NOTE

Most books on job interviewing suggest questions you can ask an employer during a job interview. Most of these questions can be adapted as informational interview questions. One such book is *101 Dynamite Questions to Ask at Your Job Interview* by Richard Fein, published by Impact Publications (Manassus Park, Virginia, 1996).

Chapter Twenty

WHAT TO ASK:

200 GREAT QUESTIONS TO CHOOSE FROM

GENERAL QUESTIONS ABOUT YOUR INTERVIEWEE'S CAREER FIELD:

1. What are the various jobs available in this field?

2. What types of training do companies offer those who enter this field?

3. In what ways is your occupation changing?

4. How is the economy affecting this industry?

5. What is the employment outlook like in your career field? How much demand is there for people in this career?

6. How quickly is the field growing?

7. What are the growth areas of this field?

8. Are you likely to have future job openings?

9. What parts of the country offer the best opportunities in this field?

10. What are the opportunities in this career like in [geographical area you are most interested in]?

11. What is the typical entry-level salary in this field?

12. What are the salary ranges for higher levels in this occupation?

13. Is there a salary ceiling?

14. Aside from such visible compensation as money, fringe benefits, travel, etc., what kinds of mental dividends (such as job satisfaction) does this career yield?

15. Is this industry heavily regulated?

16. What do you find unique about your career field?

17. From everything you've observed, what problems can you cite regarding working in this career?

18. What skills or personal characteristics do you feel contribute most to success in this industry?

19. What sacrifices have you had to make to succeed in this field, and do you feel the sacrifices were worth it?

20. When people leave this career, what are the usual reasons?

21. What are the typical entry-level job titles and functions?

22. What entry-level jobs offer the best opportunities for learning?

23. What are the most significant characteristics of this industry?

24. What trends in the field would be most likely to affect someone just entering this career now?

25. What kinds of people experience the greatest success in this field?

26. What is the most important thing that someone planning to enter this career should know?

ALL ABOUT YOUR INTERVIEWEE'S JOB:

27. What is your exact title?

28. Do other people in your company with the same job title have the same responsibilities?

29. What was your title when you first started here?

30. What precisely do you do? What are the duties/functions/responsibilities of your job?

31. What is your job like?

32. To what extent is the job what you expected?

33. How much job security do you have in this position?

34. What is a typical day like?

35. What hours do you normally work?

36. Do you have to put in much overtime or work on weekends?

37. Are the time demands of your job specific to this company, or would anyone in this career be expected to put in the same hours?

38. Do you ever bring work home with you?

39. What kinds of problems do you deal with?

40. What do you do if you can't solve a problem on your own?

41. Do you have to deal with a significant amount of conflict in this job?

Informational Interviewing

42. What systems are in place for dealing with conflict?

43. What constraints, such as time and funding, make your job more difficult?

44. What kinds of decisions do you make?

45. Describe some of the toughest situations you've faced in this job.

46. To what extent do you interact with customers/clients?

47. What percentage of your time is spent on each of your job responsibilities?

48. How does your use of time vary? Are there busy and slow times or is the work activity fairly constant?

49. Which other departments, functional units, or levels of the hierarchy do you regularly interact with?

50. How much flexibility do you have in determining how you perform your job?

51. Do you work individually or predominantly in groups or teams?

52. How are work teams or groups organized?

53. What part of this job do you personally find most satisfying? Most challenging? Least satisfying?

54. What are your personal interests and in what way does this job satisfy your interests?

55. What do you like and not like about working in this job?

56. Do you find your job exciting or boring? Why?

57. Are there aspects of your job that are repetitious?

58. Is multitasking a skill that is required for this job?

59. What projects have you worked on that have been particularly interesting?

60. What particular skills or talents are most essential to be effective in your job?

61. How did you learn these skills?

62. What are the educational requirements for this job?

63. What other types of credentials or licenses are required?

64. Is graduate school recommended? An MBA?

65. What obligations does your employer place on you outside of the ordinary work week?

66. What social obligations go along with a job in this field?

67. Are there organizations you are expected to join?

68. Are there other things you are expected to do outside of work hours?

69. How has your job affected your lifestyle?

70. To what extent does this job present a challenge in terms of juggling work and family life?

71. What are the major frustrations of this job?

72. If you could change anything about your job, what would it be?

73. Is there a great deal of turnover in this job?

74. What interests you least about the job, and what creates the most stress?

75. What is the job title of your department head or supervisor?

76. Where do you and your supervisor fit into the organizational structure?

77. How many people do you supervise?

78. How would you assess your prestige or level of status in this job? In the company?

79. If you ever left your job, what would be most likely to drive you away?

ABOUT PREPARING FOR THIS CAREER:

80. Does your work relate to any experiences or studies you had in college?

81. How well did your college experience prepare you for this job?

82. What courses have proved to be the most valuable to you in your work?

83. What courses do you wish you had taken that would have better prepared you?

84. If you were a college student again, what would you do differently to prepare for this job?

85. How important are grades or GPA for obtaining a job in this field?

86. What do you feel is the best educational preparation for this career?

87. How do you think [name of your college]'s reputation is viewed when it comes to hiring?

88. How did you prepare for this work?

89. If you were entering this career today, would you change your preparation in any way to better facilitate entry?

ABOUT YOUR INTERVIEWEE'S CAREER PATH:

90. In what way did this type of work interest you and how did you get started?

91. What was your major in college?

92. How did you get your job?

93. Did you enter this position through a formal training program?

94. What jobs and experiences have led you to your present position?

95. What did you do before you entered this occupation?

96. Which aspects of your background have been the most helpful?

97. What other jobs can you get with the same background?

98. What were the keys to your career advancement?

99. How did you get where you are and what are your long-range goals?

100. What is the job above your current job?

101. What is the next step in your career?

102. Where do you see yourself in five years?

103. If your work were suddenly eliminated, what kinds of work do you feel prepared to do?

104. If you could do things all over again, would you choose the same path for yourself? Why? What would you change?

ABOUT THE CULTURE OF YOUR INTERVIEWEE'S COMPANY OR ORGANIZATION:

105. Why did you decide to work for this company?

106. What do you like most about this company?

107. How does your company differ from its competitors?

108. Why do customers choose this company?

109. What is the company's relationship with its customers?

110. How optimistic are you about the company's future and your future with the company?

111. Has the company made any recent changes to improve its business practices and profitability?

112. What does the company do to contribute to its employees' professional development?

113. What systems are in place to enable employees to give management feedback and suggestions?

114. How does the company make use of technology for internal communication and outside marketing (e-mail, Internet, intranets, World Wide Web, videoconferencing, etc.)?

115. What other technologies are integral to the company's operation?

116. How would you describe the atmosphere at the company? Is it fairly formal or more casual and informal?

117. Do people in your department function fairly autonomously, or do they require a lot of supervision and direction?

118. What are your co-workers like?

119. How would you describe the morale of people who work here?

120. Do you participate in many social activities with your co-workers?

121. Is there a basic philosophy of the company or organization? What is it? (Is it a people-, service- or product-oriented business?)

122. What is the company's mission statement?

123. What can you tell me about the corporate culture of this company?

124. Is the company's management style executed from the top downward, or do frontline employees share in decision making?

125. Is there flexibility in work hours, vacation schedule, place of residence, telecommuting, etc.?

126. What's the dress code here? Is it conservative or casual? Does the company have dress-down or casual days?

127. Can men wear beards or long hair here?

128. What work-related values are most highly esteemed in this company (security, high income, variety, independence)?

129. What kind of training program does the company offer? Is it highly structured or more informal?

130. Does the company encourage and/or pay for employees to pursue graduate degrees? Is there a tuition-reimbursement program?

131. Does the company offer an employee discount on the products it sells?

132. What's the best thing about the company?

133. How does the company evaluate your job performance?

134. How does the company acknowledge outstanding accomplishments of its employees?

135. What kinds of accomplishments does the company reward?

136. Are there people within or outside the organization that the company holds up as heroes?

137. Does the company observe any rituals, traditions, or ceremonies?

138. What is the typical job-interview process at the company? How many interviews do candidates generally go through before being offered a position?

139. What does the company do to foster innovation and creativity?

ABOUT THE COMPANY'S NEEDS:

140. In what areas do you perceive there to be personnel gaps in this company? If the company had unlimited resources for creating new positions, in what areas do you think those positions should be created?

141. In what areas do you see the company expanding? Do you foresee the opening of new markets or greater globalization? Do you predict development of new products and/or services? Building of new facilities?

142. How can employees prepare for any planned changes at the company?

143. What obstacles do you see getting in the way of the company's profitability or growth?

144. If you needed someone to assist you in your job, what tasks would you assign to your assistant?

ABOUT OPPORTUNITIES FOR ADVANCEMENT WITHIN THIS COMPANY AND/OR FIELD:

145. How does a person progress in your field?

146. What is the highest-level job one can hold in this career?

147. What is a typical career path in this field or organization?

148. What are the advancement opportunities?

149. What is the average time an employee might stay in the job you hold?

150. How rapidly do people move to the next level in this career?

151. What incentives or disincentives are there for staying in the same job?

152. Would someone in this field need to relocate to advance in her career?

153. If I performed well at this company, where could I expect to be in five years?

SEEKING ADVICE IF YOU ARE A CAREER CHANGER:

154. My current career is _____. How easy or difficult do you think it might be to make a transition from that field to your field?

155. The skills I use the most in my current career are _____. To what extent and in what ways do you think those skills are transferable to your field?

156. What aspects of my background do you feel would be the most helpful in making the transition to your career field?

157. What aspects of my background do you feel would be the biggest obstacles to making the transition to your career field?

158. What skills needed in your career field do you think someone in my current career might be lacking and need to develop?

159. What would be the best kind of training to get to make the transition to your field?

160. What's the best way for me to get more experience in your field without taking major steps backward from the level I've progressed in my current career?

161. How do you think someone in my current field would be viewed by those with hiring power in your career? Would you personally hire someone coming from my current career field?

162. The things I like the best about my current career are _____. Will I find some of those same things if I switch to your field?

163. The things I dislike the most about my current career are _____. Will I encounter any of those same challenges in your field?

164. Do you know of any other people in your career who have made the transition to your field from my current career or a similar career? How did the transition work out?

165. I've heard that people in your field have characteristics such as _____, which I have not had the opportunity to develop in my current career. How important are those characteristics?

166. What sacrifices do you think I might have to make to switch to your career field?

167. Knowing what you know about your career field, and knowing what I would have to do to get into this field, do you think you would make the change if you were in my position? If not, can you suggest any other fields that might be more appropriate for me?

168. Would you take a brief look at my resume and suggest ways I could tailor it to make myself more marketable as I make the transition to your career field?

SEEKING GENERAL ADVICE AND REFERRALS FROM YOUR INTERVIEWEE:

169. Can you suggest some ways a person could obtain the experience necessary to enter this field?

170. What is the best way to obtain a position that will get me started in this occupation?

171. What do you wish you'd known before you entered this field?

172. What are the major qualifications for success in this occupation?

173. What are the most important skills for a position in this field?

174. What courses should I be taking?

175. How can I assess whether or not I have the skills needed for a position such as yours?

176. With the information you have about my education, skills, and experience, what other fields or jobs would you suggest I research before I make a final decision?

177. Do you know of other people whom I might contact who have jobs similar to yours?

178. Do you have any advice for someone interested in this field/job?

179. Which professional journals and publications should I be reading to learn about this career?

180. Are there any other written materials (such as company brochures) that you suggest I read?

181. Which professional organizations associated with this career should I join?

182. What kinds of experience, paid or unpaid, would you encourage for anybody pursuing a career in this field?

183. Who else do you know who uses skills similar to yours?

184. What other kinds of organizations hire people to perform the functions you do here?

185. If I am unable to obtain a position in this field, what other fields would you recommend I consider?

186. What special advice do you have for a student seeking to qualify for this position?

187. Do you have any special words of warning or encouragement as a result of your experience?

188. These are my strongest assets (skills, areas of knowledge, personality traits and values): _____. Where would they fit in this field? Where would they be helpful in this organization? Where might they fit in other fields? Where might they be helpful in other organizations?

189. What should I do to prepare myself for emerging trends and changes in this field?

190. How would you assess the experience I've had so far in terms of the requirements for entering this field?

191. What qualifications would you be looking for if you were hiring for a position such as yours?

192. What qualifications would you be looking for if you were hiring for a position subordinate to yours?

193. Do you have any written job descriptions of positions in this field/company?

194. What areas of the company would be most interested in hiring people with my background?

195. If I wanted to obtain a job here, who would the best person to contact?

196. If I wanted to obtain a job here, what would be the best way to learn of job vacancies?

197. If you were conducting a job search today, how would you go about it?

198. Would you be willing to answer more questions, by phone or in person, if I need additional advice in the future?

199. [If you feel comfortable and it seems appropriate:] Would you mind taking a look at my resume to see if you have any suggestions?

200. How would you react if you received a resume like mine for a position with this company?

FOOT NOTE

Some questions *shouldn't* be asked in an informational interview:

• **Don't ask blunt questions about the interviewee's actual salary.**

• **Don't ask for a job or ask the interviewee's help in getting you a job.**

• **Don't ask highly personal questions.**

Chapter Twenty-One

HOW TO MAXIMIZE THE INTERVIEW EXPERIENCE

ARRIVING AT THE INTERVIEW

Be sure to arrive on time for your interview. To be on the safe side, plan to arrive ten minutes early. If on the way to the interview you encounter a situation (flat tire, traffic backup, detour) that you realize will make you late for the interview, get to the nearest phone (better yet, take a cellular phone with you) and call to tell the interviewee you are running late. Ask if he would prefer to reschedule.

When you arrive, if you are greeted by a receptionist or other assistant, treat that person warmly. Such gatekeepers can be wonderful allies, and you can often learn as much from them as from your interviewees. Take your lead from the receptionist, and if small talk seems appropriate, by all means participate in the chat.

MEETING YOUR INTERVIEWEE

When you finally encounter your interviewee, greet her with a moderately firm handshake and a warm, enthusiastic smile. Thank your interviewee for taking the time to meet with you. In the interviewee's office, wait for an invitation to sit down before making yourself comfortable. Your

 FOOT NOTE

To use informational interviews to expand your network, take a list of companies you think you would like to work for. If you have enough time and good rapport with your interviewee, show him the list and ask who he knows at those companies.

conversation will probably begin with some ice-breaking chitchat. Make the most of that small talk to set yourself and your interviewee at ease.

ABSORBING YOUR SURROUNDINGS

Take in the environment at the company. How does it compare with your expectations? What would it be like to work for this organization? How quiet or noisy is it? What other establishments are nearby? Are there places to go for lunch? What's the parking situation? What's the office setup? Is it "cubicle city," or are there private offices? Do workers have windows, and if so, what kind of view do they see when they look out? Does the office seem pristine and new or shabby and dilapidated? How are people dressed? Are workers interacting, or do they keep to themselves? Does one gender predominate? Do the people seem as though they like their work, or does the atmosphere seem tense? Would you enjoy working there?

Unless your objective in the interview is to find out about the company because you are considering working there, don't be unduly influenced by the physical surroundings. If you are more interested in exploring the interviewee's job or industry than the company, realize that just because one person in this job works in an unattractive environment doesn't mean everyone with that job does. Conversely, don't conclude that a particular type of job is glamorous based on your observations of one person's workplace.

LISTENING AND OBSERVING KEENLY

Before you begin your questioning, make a brief opening statement reminding the interviewee of your objective: "I am in the process of trying to narrow down some career choices, and I am interested in finding out more about what your job (or field or company) is really like. I appreciate your taking this time with me." You may also want to share a bit about your background and aspirations. Many interviewees want to know about you so they can tailor their responses to your needs; that's why some ask to see your resume even before the interview.

As you begin asking questions, be sure to listen attentively and enthusiastically to the interviewee's responses. Look for clues to your interviewee's personality and that of his company. When appropriate, use those clues to steer the conversation toward mutual interests. Does the interviewee have lots of photos of his kids around the office? Does the interviewee display any sort of collection (for example, elephant figurines, toy soldiers, or teapots)? Is there interesting artwork in the office? Are there plants or fresh-cut flowers? Is there paraphernalia suggesting an interest in a sport? Does the interviewee's office show him to be a fan of a particular sports team? Feel free to comment about any of these clues. The interviewee will be flattered that you noticed his interests and will probably enjoy talking about them. If the interests are mutual, you can forge an even stronger bond with your interviewee. Just remember that you've asked for only a short period of the interviewee's time, so don't get bogged down talking about your mutual interest in skydiving.

While you should stick relatively close to your scripted questions, don't just become a question-spewing robot. Be businesslike and show that you take the interview seriously, but let some of your personality shine through. Discussing mutual interests is one way, but also be open to spontaneity in the conversation. If something your interviewee says makes you think of a question that's not on your list, don't hesitate to ask it. Be sure the interviewee knows how interested you are in learning about her career and how much you appreciate her information and advice. The interviewee may even start asking you questions; be sure to respond with a bright and energetic attitude. Also look for opportunities to demonstrate that you've done your homework and learned something about the company.

ENTHUSIASM IS EVERYTHING

Employers rank candidates' lack of enthusiasm in interviews as their biggest pet peeve. Interview enthusiasm is key in getting a job. The same principle applies to informational interviewing. If you are enthusiastic about learning

FOOT   NOTE

To get an even more in-depth feel for what a job or company is like, ask your interviewee if it would be possible to "shadow" her for a half or full day. Don't expect to shadow your interviewee right after your interview, but if you hit it off with her, try to arrange to come back another day and observe as she conducts a typical day's work.

about your interviewee, you will make a far more favorable impression than someone who just seems to be going through the motions. Be animated and bubbly, and the interviewee will begin thinking of you as a job candidate even though that's not why you're there.

KNOWING WHEN TO END IT

Keep an eye on the time, but be careful not to keep looking at your watch as though you're bored. As your allotted time draws to a close, make a remark such as, "I don't want to go over the thirty minutes I asked for, so let me ask you one final question." Or "Well, I promised I would take only thirty minutes of your time, so we can wrap the interview up now if you'd like." The interviewee will either accept your invitation to stop or will indicate that she is enjoying the conversation and would like it continue.

DON'T LEAVE THE INTERVIEW WITHOUT . . .

- Asking for referrals. Be sure to ask for names of other people who could give you similar information about the field and be part of your network. Once you are given names, confirm that it's okay with your interviewee for you to use his or her name when you contact the referrals. If you feel you have especially good rapport with the interviewee, you might ask if he or she would be willing to pave the way—by contacting the referral and telling him or her to expect to hear from you.
- Asking for the interviewee's business card, and if you can stay in contact.
- Thanking the interviewee. (You'll do so again in writing; see Part 4.)

FOOT  NOTE

What should you do if you are really offered a job or internship? If you're truly in an exploratory phase and are not yet sure of your career goals, you may want to wait until you've conducted more interviews before jumping at an offer. But if the timing and the job are clearly right for you, by all means take the offer (perhaps after thinking about it and discussing it with appropriate members of your network).

Chapter Twenty-Two

HOW TO TRACK AND ANALYZE YOUR INFORMATIONAL INTERVIEWS

Particularly if you conduct a large number of informational interviews, you may want to develop some sort of record-keeping system. You may very well consider your informational interviewees to be members of your network and track them the same way you track other network contacts (see Chapter 15). But you may want to keep some sort of journal or notebook to record and analyze information and impressions collected in the interviews. This information will prove extremely valuable when you later approach the interviewee or company again in search of a job instead of information, and it will enable you to demonstrate inside knowledge of each company and its needs.

You could organize your records by interviewee, or by type of job, or by company, recording key facts and personal reactions. If your main goal is to include your informational interviewees as members of your network, then organize by interviewee. If your goal is to explore careers and try to decide which path to follow, organize by job type. If your goal is to choose which companies you'd most like to apply to, organize by company. On pages 158–160 are samples of forms you could use to record information for each of these three organizational schemes. You can adapt these forms to your own needs, type them up on a word-processing program, print them out, three-hole-punch them, and place them in a binder.

Try to evaluate your informational interviews objectively. Don't automatically decide that you don't like a certain job just because you didn't have good chemistry with one of your interviewees or found the workplace drab. Consider the big picture. As you assess your experience from each interview, ask yourself some of the following questions:

- What did I get out of the informational interview experience?
- Could I have done anything to improve each individual interview?
- What did I learn overall?
- What did I learn about myself?
- Do I feel positive about what I learned?
- What did I learn about the things I value in a job and in a workplace?
- How does each job align with my own interests, abilities, and goals?
- Did one job stand out over the other(s) and provide me with clearer career direction than I had before?
- What were the positives and negatives of each interviewee's job?
- What did I learn about how to break into my preferred field?
- What did I learn about how to succeed in my preferred field?
- How do my skills/grades/experiences/personal characteristics measure up to what's required for entry or success in my preferred field?
- Do I need more training or experience to get where I want to be in my preferred field?
- Have my ideas about pursuing my preferred field changed now that I know more about it?
- Assuming I still want to pursue my original career direction, what is my strategy for seeking a job in this field?
- If I have decided against my original field, what fields am I now considering, and how will I find out if another field suits me better?
- What further information do I still need to obtain?
- What should I do next?

INFORMATIONAL INTERVIEW RECORD BY INTERVIEWEE

NAME OF INTERVIEWEE:

INTERVIEWEE'S JOB TITLE:

COMPANY NAME:

COMPANY ADDRESS:

OFFICE PHONE:

FAX:

E-MAIL:

OTHER CONTACT INFO
(HOME ADDRESS, HOME PHONE,
CELL PHONE, PAGER, ETC.):

HIGHLIGHTS OF CONVERSATION:

ADVICE GIVEN BY INTERVIEWEE:

INTERVIEWEE'S INTERESTS
(BASED ON OBSERVATIONS AND/OR
CONVERSATION):

REFERRALS PROVIDED BY INTERVIEWEE:

OTHER COMPANIES INTERVIEWEE
SUGGESTED EXPLORING:

RESUME SUGGESTIONS FROM
INTERVIEWEE:

INFORMATIONAL INTERVIEW RECORD BY JOB TYPE

TYPE/TITLE OF JOB:

INTERVIEWEE(S) HOLDING THIS JOB:

OBSERVATIONS ABOUT WORKPLACE:

TYPICAL DUTIES/FUNCTIONS/
RESPONSIBILITIES OF JOB:

TYPICAL DAY:

TYPES OF PROBLEMS:

PACE OF JOB (E.G., ALWAYS HECTIC,
GENERALLY SLOW, A COMBINATION):

DEGREE OF SUPERVISION
(IS JOB HIGHLY SUPERVISED OR ARE
WORKERS IN THIS JOB RELATIVELY
SELF-DIRECTED?):

LEVEL OF EXCITEMENT (DO INTERVIE-
WEES FIND IT EXCITING OR BORING?):

SKILLS NEEDED:

EDUCATION AND PREPARATION
NEEDED:

OUTSIDE OBLIGATIONS, EXPECTED
ORGANIZATION MEMBERSHIP:

LEVEL OF JOB IN RELATION TO REST
OF COMPANY:

NEXT LEVEL ABOVE THIS JOB:

OPPORTUNITIES FOR ADVANCEMENT:

RECOMMENDED ROUTE TO BREAK
INTO THIS TYPE OF JOB:

Informational Interviewing

INFORMATIONAL INTERVIEW RECORD BY COMPANY

NAME OF COMPANY:

TYPES OF POSITIONS AT MY LEVEL:

INTERVIEWEE(S) WORKING AT THIS COMPANY:

WORKING CONDITIONS:

CONTACT INFORMATION FOR THIS COMPANY (NAMES OF KEY HIRING MANAGERS, ADDRESSES, PHONE NUMBERS, FAX NUMBERS, PAGERS, CELL PHONES, E-MAIL ADDRESSES, WEB SITE):

CHARACTERIZATION OF PEOPLE WHO WORK HERE:

TRAINING PROGRAM(S):

ENCOURAGEMENT OR REIMBURSE-MENT FOR ADVANCED DEGREE:

REPUTATION OF COMPANY:

PROFESSIONAL DEVELOPMENT OPPORTUNITIES:

KEY PRODUCTS/SERVICES:

ADVANCEMENT OPPORTUNITIES:

COMPANY SIZE:

POSSIBILITY OF RELOCATION:

STABILITY:

SALARY STRUCTURE:

GROWTH POTENTIAL:

FRINGE BENEFITS AND PERKS:

EXPANSION PLANS (NEW MARKETS/PRODUCTS/SERVICES):

OBSERVATIONS OF PHYSICAL SURROUNDINGS:

COMPANY ORGANIZATION:

A FOOT IN THE DOOR

P A R T · F O U R

NEXT STEPS:

USING NETWORKING AND INFORMATIONAL INTERVIEWING

AS THE LAUNCH PAD FOR YOUR JOB SEARCH

Chapter Twenty-Three

THE FINE ART OF FOLLOWING UP WITH NETWORKING CONTACTS

Very few actions in the world of networking are as important as thanking those who have helped you in your job search. Anyone who provides even the minutest amount of assistance should receive a thank-you. That simple gesture of common courtesy and thoughtfulness will do more to endear you to members of your network and cement your bond with them than anything else. Because they will think of you as a conscientious and gracious person, they will be more likely to recommend you for jobs.

FOOT NOTE

You can get even more mileage out of your thank-you and follow-up efforts with some extra touches:
- **Send your contacts clippings of articles of interest to them with a sticky note attached that says, "Saw this article and thought of you."**
- **If your company produces publications that would be of interest to your contacts, have them placed on the subscription list.**
- **Consider sending amusing cartoons you've clipped, or even photos.**
- **Send a quick postcard to mention how much you enjoyed meeting a new contact. Make it a picture postcard of a local site, and you can make an inexpensive yet memorable impression.**
- **Make the saga of your job search fascinating reading as you update your contacts. Describe amusing anecdotes and interesting or famous people you may have met while networking.**
- **For someone who has been helpful beyond your wildest dreams, a grand gesture, such as sending flowers or taking them to lunch, would not be out of line.**
- **Send holiday and birthday cards.**

Conversely, your failure to thank people will do more to damage your efforts than anything else. George Moskoff, managing partner at the consulting firm Adderly Page Group, reports having spent considerable amounts of time meeting with colleagues, asking them questions, and offering advice. "Rarely do I get a note thanking me for my time," he writes in *Manage* magazine. "It hurts."

Corresponding with your network contacts keeps your name in front of them so they may think of you when an opportunity comes up that would be a good fit for you. Sending thank-you and follow-up letters also keeps members of your network informed of your progress. Tell those who've given you advice about the results of your following the advice. Moskoff notes that letting members of your network in on the process of your job hunt can be even more important than making contact initially. He suggests letting your contacts know "what you're doing, whom you're interviewing with, how the interviews went."

A thank-you to your network contacts can be in the form of a handwritten social note or greeting card. It can also be a typed business letter. You can send thank-yous by e-mail for immediacy, although it's a nice idea to follow those up with a "hard copy" note sent through the mail. At the end of your job search, when you've found a wonderful new job, send a thank you to everyone who helped in any way. Following are some sample thank-you notes:

THANK YOU FOR HELP PROVIDED BY A NETWORK CONTACT

Dear Jackie:

I'm writing to thank you for agreeing to be a member of my personal "network." This is an important time in my life as I take the plunge to change careers, and I truly value the advice of professionals like you who know the physical therapy field so well.

I especially appreciate your offer to coach me in interviewing for a job in this field. As an insider, you can provide interviewing tips that very few others can.

Jackie, thanks again for your willingness to help me launch this next phase of my career. I will be sure to keep you informed of my progress.

Don't hesitate to let me know if you think of any additional suggestions or names of people I should contact.

Sincerely,

[Name]

UPDATE ON PROGRESS

Dear Mr. Byron:

I just wanted to drop a line to thank you for your continued support and to keep you abreast of recent progress in my job search.

I've had half a dozen promising interviews in the past few weeks. No offers yet—but three of the firms have invited me back for second interviews, so I'm very excited!

I could never have come this far without your encouragement, Mr. Byron. I greatly appreciate all you've done for me. You will be among the very first to hear the news when I land my dream job! Please let me know if you think of anyone else I should be talking to.

Best regards,

[Name]

FOLLOW-UP ON ADVICE

Dear Ms. Allyson:

I just had to write to let you know that your suggestion to join my local chapter of Women in Engineering really paid off! Thank you so much!

I went to my first meeting earlier this week and met some wonderful women. I even landed an interview with Bernadette Donaldson. I will be sure to let you know how it goes.

Joining this group was a great suggestion, and I wouldn't have thought of it on my own. I am so thankful to have people like you to guide me in my career. I certainly welcome any additional suggestions you might have or names of people who might become part of my network. Please also keep me in mind if you learn of anyone in the industry who could use someone with my skills and experience.

Yours,

[Name]

SHARING INFORMATION

Dear Dr. Dorchester:

I just wanted to touch base with you and say hello. My job search continues to be productive, thanks in large part to your many suggestions.

I've just learned that Dr. Joseph Reedy will be speaking in town next month. I know you have followed his theories closely, so I wanted to make sure you were aware of his upcoming lecture. I've enclosed an article on Dr. Reedy, which includes details about the lecture.

Thank you again, Dr. Dorchester, for all your support. I hope I see you at the lecture.

Sincerely,

[Name]

THANK YOU FOR INFORMATIONAL INTERVIEW

Dear Mrs. Mays:

I can't thank you enough for taking time out of your busy schedule so I could conduct an informational interview with you. I learned a great deal from my time with you.

While many aspects of the hydrogeology field are quite different from what I previously thought, I am more excited than ever about the profession.

Mrs. Mays, you were extremely generous with both your time and information. You have contributed immeasurably to my career development, and I thank you very much. I especially appreciate your suggestions for tuning up my resume. I'm also glad you invited me to keep in touch and apprise you of my career progress, because I fully intend to do so!

Cordially,

[Name]

THANK YOU AT END OF JOB SEARCH

Dear Sam,

I wanted you to be among the first to know that my job search has ended! After a lengthy search and several months of interviews, I accepted a position with Polymers Unlimited, an international corporation headquartered in Columbia, South Carolina. Even though the company is quite large, the marketing department is made up of just three of us.

I really have a lot of fun there. I am responsible for all of the marketing communications. I love it. I know I am going to learn so much; the firm is great about arranging additional training for employees. The company will be sending me to newsletter seminars, software classes, you name it. I believe I have really found what I love to do.

You were so instrumental in my search, and I can never thank you enough. You gave me invaluable ideas and advice, and so many referrals. I am very grateful.

I have enclosed a business card for my new position. Please keep in touch, and if there's ever anything I can do for you, don't hesitate to call on me!

Yours,

[Name]

FOOT NOTE

At the end of your job search, throw a big party and invite your whole network, suggests Guy Felton on his networking Web site. What better way to thank everyone —and your party might just provide networking opportunities for others.

Chapter Twenty-Four

USING NAME-DROPPING REFERRAL COVER LETTERS TO GET THE MOST OUT OF YOUR NETWORK OF CONTACTS

Anytime a member of your network gives you the name of someone who might be able to offer you a job, you have the opportunity to write what I have dubbed the Referral Cover Letter. A referral cover letter, accompanied by your resume, is more likely to result in an interview than almost any other kind of cover letter. Why? Because when you drop the name of someone both you and the recipient of the letter know, you get the recipient's attention. Further, the recipient is more inclined to interview you to avoid seeming rude to your mutual acquaintance. That's just one reason networking is so valuable; the more people there are in your network, the more opportunities you will have to write this extremely effective type of cover letter.

Another type of referral cover letter is the self-referral, in which the person who has "referred" you to the letter's recipient is none other than yourself. The recipient is someone you've met in some context, such as in an informational interview, social situation, or professional meeting. It could also be someone you haven't met but have corresponded with or talked to over the phone. You use the self-referral cover letter to remind the recipient of your acquaintance. Following are some samples:

 FOOT NOTE

To learn me about how to write a cover letter, see my previous books, *Dynamic Cover Letters: How to Sell Yourself to an Employer by Writing a Letter That Will Get Your Resume Read, Get You an Interview, and Get You the Job* and *Dynamic Cover Letters for New Graduates* (both published by Ten Speed Press, Berkeley, California).

COLLEGE STUDENT REFERRAL LETTER

Dear Ms. Timothy:

Your colleague, Jack Waycross, suggested I contact you about the possibility of a full-time position with SpringSweet. As a senior student earning a Bachelor of Business Administration degree from the University of Minnesota, I am ready to make a meaningful contribution to the SpringSweet marketing and sales team.

Both my academic career and employment experience have prepared me well for a career with SpringSweet. My challenging and competitive academic program has included such unique courses as consumer behavior, channels and physical distribution, leadership seminars, and production and operation management. In addition to my schooling, I have worked in the marketing department of Daisy Products, where I added to my sales and marketing experience.

My previous employers can verify that I am an enthusiastic and effective salesman. During my summers at Daisy, I consistently maintained the highest seasonal sales totals. In addition to my previous job experiences, my position as a member of the Minnesota men's soccer team has provided me with significant leadership skills, as well as the ability to work well with a team.

Because you undoubtedly know that a letter and resume can convey only a limited sense of a person's qualifications, I believe it would be productive for us to meet in person, so that I may present my credentials more completely. I will contact you in a few days to arrange a meeting. Should you wish to reach me before that, my number is 555-1927. Please feel free to leave a message if I am not available. I am looking forward to meeting with you.

Thank you for your time and consideration.

Sincerely,

Max Bonwit

ESTABLISHED JOB SEEKER REFERRAL LETTER

Dear Mr. Sabovsky,

John Winterrowd and I have been talking about how my skills might fit in at InfoSource. He said he'd discussed with you the possibility that I might assist you in your customer service department, so I wanted to introduce myself and tell you a little of what I've done since working with John at GalleryPlex.

I have extensive customer service experience in the high-energy _____ field and I plan to make customer service my life's work. My abilities to communicate effectively, handle customer problems quickly and personably, and work well in high-stress situations have helped me to succeed in every position I have held.

In addition, I have excellent organizational and writing skills, as my former employers can attest. I am currently training to enhance my computer skills, and I have the desire and competence to learn quickly.

I know you won't regret giving me an opportunity to show you what I can do. I am very interested in working for your company, and I believe that you will be happy with my performance.

I will call you in a few days to arrange a time when we can meet in person.

Sincerely,

Maggie Seaborn

SELF-REFERRAL LETTER BASED ON A SOCIAL ENCOUNTER

Dear Mr. Jackson,

As you may recall, we met at Louise Baptiste's Memorial Day barbecue. I came away from our stimulating conversation about trends in the media thinking that I would love to work with you. When Louise suggested that I apply for the available position in your public relations department, I was thrilled with the idea. It would be wonderful to work for your prestigious company, and I am ready to join your outstanding team.

I know that you need someone who is enthusiastic and task oriented, and I am uniquely qualified for the job. Some people are great team performers, while others are better working on their own—I am both!

My success in setting up media features and interviews for San Diego State Bank and the bank's stellar reputation in the media show that I am a top-notch publicist. My position as the mayor's public information officer gave me the chance to organize events and handle media requests in a high-pressure environment.

I am fluent in Spanish, which, as you know, is imperative to your industry in Southern California. I also have excellent computer skills, as I work daily with the Microsoft Office programs and the Internet.

As you can see, I am a dynamic person with a passionate interest in your company. My background has provided me with the skills to be an asset to your company. My outgoing personality, accompanied by my profit- and task-oriented work style, makes me an excellent choice for the job.

I will contact your secretary this week for an interview. I look forward to speaking with you again. Thank you for your time and consideration; I hope to see you soon.

Sincerely,

Sally Ringo

REFERRAL LETTER BASED ON AN INFORMATIONAL INTERVIEW

Dear Mr. Newcom:

Last October I conducted an enlightening informational interview with Krista Tillikum, your human resources associate director. She suggested I contact you when the time came for me to actively seek a human resources position.

I am a highly motivated, hard-working person with a track record to prove it. I have recently graduated from Fairleigh-Dickinson with a degree in business administration and I am eager to put my education to work in a job such as the human resources generalist position you have open.

In addition to my education, I have a five-year history of steady advancement with the university libraries, where I participated in the interviewing, hiring, and training of more than one hundred individuals. I am looking forward to proving myself in the field of human resources, where I hope to find a satisfying and productive career.

From my work experience, I know the value of a good employee. Previous employers will affirm that they have entrusted me with major responsibility and that I adapt well to change. I have a strong work ethic and I am confident that I will be an asset to your company.

I am available for an interview at your convenience. I may be reached at 201-555-8747 during the day or 201-555-1176 in the evenings.

Thank you for your consideration.

Sincerely,

Gayle McNerney

SELF-REFERRAL LETTER BASED ON AN INFORMATIONAL INTERVIEW

Dear Ms. McCloud:

I'm sure you remember my conducting an informational interview with you last November. The insight you provided into the interior design world was invaluable to me, and I thank you again for giving so generously of your time and information. I'm now starting my job search in earnest and would like to meet with you again to discuss the possibility of joining your firm.

In my most recent position as an architectural assistant, I headed up activities ranging from complete coordination and production of construction drawings to space planning and design development. I met with clients, identified their needs, and executed their space plans in New York and Philadelphia. As my previous employer can attest, my work was accurate and detail oriented.

I've been impressed by the exceptional work McCloud Interiors does, and I'm convinced that I can enhance the firm's success.

Ms. McCloud, I believe my qualifications are an excellent fit with the position and that it would be mutually beneficial for us to meet. I will call you early next week to set up an appointment for an interview.

Sincerely,

Marty Panich

SELF-REFERRAL LETTER BASED ON AN ENCOUNTER AT A PROFESSIONAL ORGANIZATION

Dear Mr. Morris:

I enjoyed speaking with you at the American Accounting Association convention and hearing your insights into exactly what is involved in this type of career and what skills are needed. Based on what you told me, I'm convinced my skills and experience are a perfect fit for an audit manager position.

I plan to relocate to Austin this summer and my experience has prepared me well for a career in accounting. In addition to what I have learned in my continuing-education accounting courses, I have acquired advanced computer skills in the programs Excel, Peachtree, and QuickBooks and others. My long-term educational goals include the completion of the additional courses necessary to obtain a Master of Accountancy degree and CPA certification.

My experience as an accounting manager further qualifies me for a job in your company. I have maintained a position with one company for several years in which I had full responsibility for all accounts. This position has allowed me to increase my effectiveness in managing accounts while providing exemplary results. My previous employers can affirm that I am extremely motivated and dependable under pressure.

I am confident that I would be an asset to Morris and Associates. My background provides me with qualifications that are an excellent fit with the needs of this position. In addition, my strong dedication to achieving excellence would certainly help your company to prosper.

Mr. Morris, I am eager to meet with you again. I will contact you next week to arrange for an interview at your convenience. In the meantime, please feel free to contact me at my campus number listed above.

Thank you for your time and consideration.

Sincerely,

Amy Parkinson

SELF-REFERRAL LETTER BASED ON PREVIOUS CORRESPONDENCE

Dear Mr. Richards:

Back in January, before I located to Rochester from Great Neck, I wrote to you about the possibility of employment with your organization. You responded with an extremely encouraging letter. You said that with my qualifications, I should have no difficulty finding a job here.

I'm happy to say you were right. I'm working as the legal affairs coordinator in the Department of Public Works. Having gotten such a warm reception from you in your very kind letter, I thought you might like to know that I am here in Rochester and am enhancing my ability to make a contribution to an organization such as yours.

I am well versed in cutting-edge environmental issues. And, having worked as a lobbyist for the Atlantic Coast Preservation League, I am also highly adept in lobbying state, local, and federal governmental entities on important environmental issues.

Mr. Richards, I have enclosed some of my position papers. I believe it would be constructive for us to meet. I would like to be considered for a lobbyist position. I'm convinced that my qualifications and your needs are a perfect match.

I'll check in with you at the Environmental Awards luncheon next week. You may also wish to reach me; during business hours, you can call 555-4800 or leave a message on my home machine at 555-2010.

Thank you for your consideration, and thanks again for your wonderful letter in January.

Cordially,

Joshua Abrahms

SELF-REFERRAL LETTER BASED ON
A PHONE CONVERSATION

Dear Ms. Bowman:

I thoroughly enjoyed speaking with you on the phone last week. When you informed me of the upcoming vacancy in your travel services department, I was thrilled. My solid experience in customer service makes me a perfect candidate for the Travel Counselor position.

My background in the corporate travel industry has helped me to become extremely adept at making optimal travel arrangements, providing business services of all kinds, and functioning as a productive team member. I understand the needs of the business traveler who seeks practical, yet comfortable, arrangements.

My strong organizational skills would serve me well in saving clients money and identifying the most efficient and enjoyable means of travel. My former employers will attest that I work extremely well and produce timely results under pressure, and that I possess exceptional telephone and customer-service skills.

I am convinced that I would be an asset to your team. I will contact you in ten days to arrange an appointment for us to meet in person. Should you wish to speak to me in the meantime, you may reach me (414) 555-2010.

Once again, it was wonderful to talk with you, and thank you for considering my qualifications.

Sincerely,

Misha Gabriel

Chapter Twenty-Five

THE NEEDS-FULFILLMENT COVER LETTER

One of the most powerful aspects of networking, and especially informational interviewing, is the opportunity they afford to find out about an employer's needs. Every need discovered is an opportunity. During your networking and informational interviewing, be alert to problems you could solve, gaps you could fill, situations you could improve. After all, employers look for those who can fulfill their needs. Networking and informational interviewing give you an opportunity to uncover and tap into an organization's needs—often even before the company has begun to address the need. It's a priceless technique because not only can you describe yourself as the perfect person to meet the need, but you can make yourself a shining star in the employer's eyes for showing awareness of and concern for the firm's well-being. Following are examples of this approach:

Dear Mr. Zwanger:

I enjoyed chatting with you last week at the Manufacturers Association dinner. I recall our discussion about the difficulties you've been having in meeting your production schedules. I've been giving considerable thought to your dilemma and have come up with some ideas. I wondered if we might be able to get together so I can share my thoughts with you.

As you know, I am foreman at Supplee and Company. I've developed a highly effective scheduling system; we have not missed a deadline in seven years. I'd really like to bring this scheduling success to Eastwood.

I'll give you a call next week to see if we can arrange a time to continue our conversation.

Sincerely,

Sid Ross

Dear Ms. Stevens:

Your co-worker Andrea Kirkwood suggested I contact you about a position in your real estate office. When I interviewed Ms. Kirkwood six months ago to obtain information about a career in real estate, she mentioned that the agency would like to establish a Web presence. I'd like to combine my interest in real estate with my knowledge of Web page design and HTML programming to help create a Webmaster position in your office. I've sketched out some preliminary ideas of what your Web page might look like, and I'd love to get together and show them to you.

While I have recently begun training for my real estate license, I've been an art director/graphic artist at PacificWeb for more than two years. I began my Internet-design career by working with numerous local and national companies. With these assignments, I've use my creative problem-solving abilities to create Web sites that are informative, eye-catching, and easy to use.

I am convinced that you would love my ideas for your Web site. I will contact you in ten days to arrange a time when we can meet. Should you have any questions before my call, please don't hesitate to contact me. Thanks so much for your consideration.

Cordially,

Cynthia Phillips

This list of resources is not exhaustive, but it provides a good sampling of networking tools and organizations. The categories of resources, in which items are arranged alphabetically, include

- General networking organizations
- General professional organizations and associations
- Women's networking and professional organizations
- Minority networking and professional organizations
- Internet networking resources
- Print and Internet networking publications.

Where available, a mailing address, phone number, fax number, Web site address, and e-mail address are provided for each resource. Many resources require a fee or dues. Descriptions of resources have been, for the most part, provided by the organizations themselves. Keep in mind that Web sites are subject to change; they frequently change addresses or cease to exist. If you come across an outdated Web address here, check for updates at the "A Foot in the Door Networking Resources" section of the Quintessential Careers Web site at *http://www.quintcareers.com/networking.html*.

NETWORKING ORGANIZATIONS

All Cities Resource Group
Web site: *http://allcities.org/index.html*
A California organization that sponsors a series of Networking Business Groups that meet monthly. The membership comprises high-caliber professionals who have a common client base. The purpose of the group is to develop relationships among the members. Based on these relationships, members have opportunities to assist each other with referrals to their customers and clients.

Exec-U-Net, Inc.
25 Van Zant St.
Norwalk, CT 06855
Phone: 800-637-3126
Fax: 203-851-5177
Web site: *http://www.clickit.com/touch/execnet/hidden/senior.htm*
E-mail: *execunet@execunet.com*
Exec-U-Net is a career management information service and career advancement networking organization exclusively for executives and senior professionals with yearly salaries in excess of $75,000. Started in 1988, it is a membership organization that helps executives enhance their networking and take control of their careers.

Five O'Clock Club
300 E. 40 St. 6L
New York, NY 10016
Phone: 212-286-4500
Web site: *http://www.fiveoclockclub.com/*
A national career counseling network with certified career counselors across the United States.

Forty Plus
Web site:
http://www.fortyplus.org/chapters.html
(Forty Plus apparently does not have a national Web site, but this California site lists local chapters around the country.)
A nonprofit organization that provides professional job search programs, networking opportunities, and a wide variety of resources to members, who are executives, managers, and professionals.

Networking Institute
505 Waltham St.
West Newton, MA 02165
Phone: 617-965-3340
Fax: 617-965-2341
Contact: Jessica Lipnack, executive officer
Promotes the establishment of networks to help people work together more effectively. Offers consulting services, educational materials, seminars, and workshops.

Networks Unlimited, Inc.
337 44th St.
Brooklyn, NY 11220
Contact: Alina Novak, president
Composed of individuals in business or the professions who are interested in furthering the networking process. Conducts monthly educational meetings on topics of interest. Maintains videotape library on the basics of networking and lends out copies of speeches on networks and networking. Bestows awards; offers placement services; operates speakers' bureau; compiles statistics.

Powerlunch!
c/o The Employment Support Center
900 Massachusetts Ave. NW, No. 444
Washington, DC 20001
Phone: 202-783-4747
Contact: Ellie Wegener, executive officer
Seeks to enhance networking capabilities by matching an individual seeking a specific type of information with an expert in that field. Capitalizes on the concept "it's not what you know, but who you know." Activities are currently limited to the Washington, D.C., area; the organization plans to expand nationally.

Toastmasters International
P.O. Box 9052
Mission Viejo, CA 92690
Phone: 949-858-8255
Fax: 949-858-1207
Web site: *http://www.toastmasters.org/*
While not strictly a networking organization, Toastmasters enables members to build confidence by speaking to groups and working with others in a supportive environment.

U.S. Junior Chamber of Commerce (Jaycees)
4 W. 21st St.
Tulsa, OK 74114-1116
Phone: 918-584-2481
Fax: 918-584-4422

Customer Service Hotline: 800-JAY-CEES
Web site: *http://www.usjaycees.org/*
The Jaycees describe themselves as "the organization of choice for men and women 21–39 years of age who want the best opportunities for leadership development, volunteerism and community service."

GENERAL PROFESSIONAL ORGANIZATIONS AND ASSOCIATIONS

Since thousands of professional organizations are available, the best resources in this area are tools that help you find professional organizations and associations in your field.

Associations on the Net
Web site: *http://www.ipl.org/ref/AON/*
This site lists organizations that have a Web presence, enabling you to explore groups you might want to join.

Gateway to Associations Online
Web site: *http://www.asaenet.org/Gateway/OnlineAssocSlist.html*
Maintained by the American Society of Association Executives, this site provides a comprehensive directory to Web sites to business and professional associations.

associationcentral.com
Web site: *http://www.associationcentral.com*
This Web site is useful for locating professional societies, trade associations, or other member organizations. The site's scope of organizations is somewhat wider than the sites devoted exclusively to professional organizations.

Encyclopedia of Associations
To find organizations and associations off-line, consult this library reference book, published by Gale Research, Incorporated.

WOMEN'S NETWORKING AND PROFESSIONAL ORGANIZATIONS

NETWORKING ORGANIZATIONS

Advancing Women
Web site: *http://www.advancingwomen.com/*
E-mail: *publisher@advancingwomen.com*
This International Network for Women in the Workplace Web site highlights issues for the working woman. Includes an on-line career center, Today's Women's News feature, forums for discussion, links for networking with international women, personal services resources, and links to similar sites.

American Association of University Women
1111 16th St. NW
Washington, DC 20036
Phone: 202-785-7700
Web site: *http://www.aauw.org/*
A national organization that promotes education and equity for all women and girls.

American Business Women's Association
9100 Ward Pkwy.
Kansas City, MO 64114-0728
Phone: 816-361-6621
Call the national headquarters for local contacts.

Business and Professional Women USA
2012 Massachusetts Ave. NW
Washington, DC 20036
Phone: 202-293-1200
Web site: *http://www.bpwusa.org/*
Hosts meetings to discuss issues such as equity, job advancement, and networking.

National Association of Women Business Owners
1511 K St. NW, Suite 1100
Washington, DC 20005
Phone: 202-638-5322
Web site:
http://www.nawbo.org/nawbo/nawbostart.nsf
Leadership training and a network for women who have been in business for themselves for more than eight years.

National Women's Political Caucus
1211 Connecticut Ave. NW, Suite 425
Washington, DC 20036
Phone: 202-785-1100
Web site: *http://www.nwpc.org/*
Leadership and campaign-training programs.

Women's Information Network
1511 K St. NW, Suite 635
Washington, DC 20005
Phone: 202-347-2827
Web site: *http://www.winon-line.org/*
A Democratic group that serves mostly younger women. Features a job center and a well-reputed networking event, "Women Opening Doors for Women," in which high-level professional women share their experiences at informal dinners.

National Association for Female Executives (NAFE)
135 W. 50th St.
New York, NY 10020
Phone: 212-445-6100
Web site: *http://www.nafe.com/*
E-mail: *nafe@nafe.com*
With some 250,000 members nationwide

and abroad, the National Association for Female Executives (NAFE) is the nation's largest association for businesswomen. NAFE provides resources and services through education, networking, and public advocacy to empower its members to achieve career success and financial security. The Web site provides information about NAFE, its membership benefits and services, and NAFE networks around the country. It also includes articles and information about business and management, selected articles from NAFE's *Executive Female* magazine, and links to business-related sites.

PROFESSIONAL ORGANIZATIONS

A limited selection of women's professional organizations is provided here. To locate professional organizations specifically for women, use the Gateway to Associations Online search engine at *http://www.asaenet.org/Gateway/OnlineAssocS list.html*. This search engine has a pull-down menu that enables you to select "women" as one of the search criteria. The Women's Enterprise Web site at *http://www.womens-enterprise.com/network.htm* contains a lengthy list of women's professional and networking organizations (with phone numbers only).

American Medical Women's Association
801 N. Fairfax St., Suite 400
Alexandria, VA 22314
Phone: 703-838-0500
This association serves female health professionals.

American Woman's Society of Certified Public Accountants (AWSCPA)
401 N. Michigan Ave.
Chicago, IL 60611
Phone: 312-664-6610, 800-AWSCPA-1
Fax: 312-527-6783
Web site: *http://www.awscpa.org/*

E-mail: *admin@awscpa.org*

The American Woman's Society of Certified Public Accountants is devoted exclusively to the support and professional development of women CPAs. The society also addresses gender equity, the glass ceiling, and work and family issues. To accomplish its mission, AWSCPA offers in-depth support in six areas, including networking. AWSCPA's Web site has information about meetings and conferences as well as current job opportunities. Some areas of the site are open to members only.

American Women in Radio and Television

1650 Tysons Blvd., Suite 200
McLean, VA 22102
Phone: 703-506-3290
Serves women working in electronic media and related fields and offers a job-fax service.

Association for Women in Communications

c/o1733 20th St. NW, Suite 301
Washington, DC 20009
Phone: 202-973-2136
Offers a mentor program and an annual career day.

Association for Women in Computing

41 Sutter St., Suite 1006
San Francisco, CA 94104
Phone: 415-905-4663
E-mail: *awc@acm.org*
Web site: *http://www.awc-hq.org/*
Serves programmers, analysts, technical writers, and entrepreneurs. Contact the national headquarters for local information.

Association for Women in Development

1511 K St. NW, Suite 825
Washington, DC 20005
Phone: 202-628-0440
Serves women working on international-development issues.

Association for Women in Science (AWIS)

1200 New York Ave. NW, Suite 650
Washington, DC 20005
Phone: 202-326-8940; 800-886-AWIS
Web site: *http://www.serve.com/awis*
E-mail: *awis@awis.org*
The Association for Women in Science (AWIS) is a nonprofit organization dedicated to achieving equity and full participation for women in science, mathematics, engineering, and technology. AWIS has more than 5,000 members in fields spanning the life and physical sciences, mathematics, social science, and engineering. Events at the 76 local chapters across the country facilitate networking among women scientists at all levels and in all career paths.

Association of Women in International Trade

P.O. Box 65962
Washington, DC 20035
Phone: 202-785-9842
Web site: *http://www.embassy.org/wiit/*
Monthly events with speakers, periodic seminars on trade topics, and a job bank.

Federally Employed Women

1400 I St. NW, Suite 425
Washington, DC 20005-2252
Phone: 202-898-0994
Web site: *http://216.51.10.199/*
E-mail: *execdir@few.org*
Serves women in all levels of the federal government, including the military. Also offers a mentor program and seminars on policy and legislative processes.

Financial Women International

200 N. Glebe Rd., Suite 814
Arlington, VA 22203-3128
Phone: 703-807-2007
Web address: *http://www.fwi.org/*
Formerly known as the National Association of Bank Women, FWI serves women in banking and financial services.

International Alliance for Women in Music

Department of Music
George Washington University NW
Washington, DC 20052
Phone: 202-994-6338
Web site:
http://music.acu.edu/www/iawm/home.html
Serves composers, conductors, performers, and music lovers; provides venues for female artists to perform; and helps promote their shows.

National Association of Insurance Women

1847 E. 15th St.
Tulsa, OK 74104
Phone: 800-766-NAIW
Web site: *http://www.naiw.org/*
E-mail: *National@naiw.org*
Provides opportunities for women in the insurance industry to expand their circles of business contacts and knowledge through association activities such as state meetings, regional conferences, and a national convention. Call the national office to locate local chapters.

National Association for Women in Education

1325 18th St. NW, Suite 210
Washington, DC 20036-6511
Phone: 202-659-9330
Web site: *http://www.nawe.org/*
Serves women in education, administration, teaching, and research positions, mostly in higher education.

National Network of Commercial Real Estate Women

1201 Wakarusa Dr., Suite 1A
Lawrence, KS 66049
Phone: 913-832-1808
Web site: *http://www.nncrew.org/*
For women working in all facets of commercial real estate. Call the national headquarters for local contacts.

Organization of Women in International Trade (OWIT)

Web site: *http://www.owit.org/*
E-mail: *ewhalley@worldnet.att.net*
The Organization of Women in International Trade (OWIT) is a nonprofit professional organization designed to promote women doing business in international trade by providing networking and educational opportunities. Members include women and men doing business in all facets of international trade, including finance, public relations, government, freight forwarding, international law, agriculture, sales and marketing, import/export, logistics, and transportation. The Web site contains information about conferences, events, chapters in the United States and around the world, as well as a job bank.

Society of Women Engineers

120 Wall St.
New York, NY 10005
Phone: 212-509-9577
Web site: *http://www.swe.org/*
Contact the national headquarters for local contacts.

Women in Advertising and Marketing

4200 Wisconsin Ave. NW
Washington, DC 20016
Phone: 301-369-7400
Monthly networking dinners, speakers bureau, and a job bank.

Women in Housing and Finance

6712 Fisher Ave.
Falls Church, VA 22046
Phone: 703-536-5112
Monthly luncheons, a job bank, professional development, and special-interest groups on insurance, securities, and technology.

Women in International Security
Center for International and Security
Studies
University of Maryland
College Park, MD 20742
Phone: 301-405-7612
Web site: *http://www.puaf.umd.edu/wiis/*
WIIS (pronounced "wise") is dedicated to
enhancing opportunities for women
working in foreign and defense policy. An
international, nonprofit, nonpartisan net-
work and educational program, WIIS is
open to both women and men at all
stages of their careers.

**Women in Technology
International (WITI)**
12015 Lee-Jackson Hwy.
Fairfax, VA 22033
Phone: 703-267-3565
Web site: *http://www.witi.com/*
WITI's goal is to empower its constituents
by providing access to people and content

that are relevant to the issues faced by
women in technology.

Women's Caucus for the Arts
P.O. Box 1498, Canal St. Station
New York, NY 10013
Phone: 212-634-0007
Web site: *http://www.nationalwca.com/*
Has established a national network through
research, exhibitions, conferences, and
honor awards for achievement. Call the
national headquarters for local contacts.

**Women's National Book
Association**
3101 Ravensworth Pl.
Alexandria, VA 22302
Phone: 703-578-4023
http://www.wbna-books.org/
Serves women in publishing, writing, and
editing, as well as those who have an
interest in books. Offers professional-
development programs.

MINORITY NETWORKING ORGANIZATIONS AND RESOURCES

As with women's resources, a limited selection of minority networking/
professional organizations and Web sites is provided here. To locate
organizations specifically for minorities, select "minority" in the pull-
down menu on the Gateway to Associations Online search engine at
http://www.asaenet.org/Gateway/OnlineAssocSlist.html.

Africamvillage
10 West Ashmead Place South
Philadelphia, PA 19144
Phone: 215-848-0852
Web site: *http://www.africamvillage.com/
africamvillage/home.html*
E-mail: *yourhost@africamvillage.com*
Web site features an Afrocentric mall, a de-
velopment center, and on-line networking.

African American Business
Web site: *http://www.aabl.com/*
A directory and communication center
for African American-owned businesses
and organizations. Offers business links,
on-line shopping, an employment center
and a news magazine.

African American Internetwork
Web site: *http://www.afamnet.com/*
A Web site promoting on-line, interactive
communications among African Americans.

African Grapevine, Inc.

Web site: *http://www.africangrapevine.com/*
African Grapevine, Inc. (AGI) is a community-based organization that focuses on building financial wealth in the black community, Afrocentric networking, community services and markets and professional development.

Black Career Women

P.O. Box 19332
Cincinnati, OH 45219
Web site: *http://www.bcw.org/*
National professional development organization.

HISPANIC Online

Web site: *http://www.hisp.com/*
An on-line forum on the Web and America Online for Latinos living in the United States. HISPANIC Online offers chat rooms, message boards and news, events, and issues of interest to the Latino community.

International Society of African Scientists

P.O. Box 9209
Wilmington, DE 19809
Web site: *http://www.dca.net/isas/*
Promotes the advancement of science and technology among people of African descent.

LatinoLink

601 Van Ness Ave., #E-3309
San Francisco. CA 94102
Phone: 415-357-1172
Fax: 415-543-4878
E-mail: *latino@latinolink.com*
Web site: *http://www.latinolink.com/*
Includes chat areas, bulletin boards, and a job bank.

Minority Business Network

Web site: *http://www.mbnglobal.com/*
Covers minority business and world affairs as well as emerging international markets.

National Association of Asian American Professionals

c/o NAAAP-Chicago
P.O. Box 81138
Chicago, IL 60681
Hotline: 773-918-2454
Web site: *http://www.naaap.org/*
E-mail: *naaap@naaap.org*
A national network of metropolitan organizations dedicated to serving the needs of Asian American professionals across the United States. Promotes Pan-Asian unity through fellowship and professional networking.

National Association of Black Accountants, Inc.

7249-A Hanover Pkwy.
Greenbelt, MD 20770
Phone: 301-474-NABA
Fax: 301-474-3114
Web site: *http://www.wam.umd.edu/~mckinney/Organizations/NABA/NABA.html*
E-mail: Paul Lancaster at *los@wam.umd.edu*
Promotes greater participation by minorities in the accounting profession.

National Association of Negro Business and Professional Women's Clubs

1806 New Hampshire Ave. NW
Washington, DC 20009
Phone: 202-483-4206
Web site: *http://www.afrika.com/nanbpwc/*
Offers a job line, economic-development opportunities, and community-service projects.

National Black MBA Association

180 N. Michigan Ave., Suite 1400
Chicago, IL 60601
Phone: 312-236-BMBA (2622)
Fax: 312-236-4131
Web site: *http://nbmbaa.org/*
E-mail: *mail@nbmbaa.org*
Business organization that works to create economic and intellectual wealth for the black community.

National Black Programmers Coalition

Web site: *http://nbpcinc.org/*
E-mail: *info@nbpcinc.org*

An organization of professionals who have united forces to promote positive ideas and education, and to generate resources, that will enhance the radio and record industry for the betterment of its members.

National Council of Negro Women, Inc.

633 Pennsylvania Ave. NW
Washington, DC 20004
Phone: 202-737-0120
Web site: *http://www.ncnw.com/*
E-mail: *info@ncnw.com*

A nonprofit organization that works at the national, state, local, and international levels in pursuit of the goal to "leave no one behind" and improve quality of life for women, children, and families.

National Federation of Black Women Business Owners

1500 Massachusetts Ave. NW, Suite 34
Washington, DC 20005
Phone: 202-833-3450
Support, networking, and information clearinghouse.

National Hispanic Business Association

1712 E. Riverside Dr., #208
Austin, TX 78741
Phone: 512-495-9511
Fax: 512-495-9730
Web site: *http://www.nhba.org/*
A national network of students and alumni whose mission is to address educational and business issues related to Hispanics.

National Organization of Black Law Enforcement Executives

4609 Pinecrest Office Park Dr., Suite F
Alexandria, VA 22312-1442
Phone: 703-658-1529
Fax: 703-658-9479

Web site: *http://www.noblenatl.org/*
E-mail: *noble@noblenatl.org*
Offers training in cultural diversity, community policing, and law enforcement issues.

National Society of Black Engineers

Web site: *http://www.nsbe.org/*
Membership, conventions, career fairs, pre-college activities, and other helpful programs are sponsored by the NSBE.

National Society of Hispanic MBAs

8204 Elmbrook, Suite 235
Dallas, TX 75247
Phone: 877-467-4622 (toll-free)
Fax: 214-267-1626
Web site: *http://www.nshmba.org/*
E-mail: *info@nshmba.org*
Provides career networking opportunities for Hispanic business professionals.

Native Web Community Center

Web site:
http://www.nativeweb.org/community/
This Web site's purpose is to bring together indigenous peoples around the world by providing the tools and resources needed to communicate. Lists news, events, jobs, and other community-oriented resources. E-mail lists (with archives), chat boards, and more are planned for the future.

Networking Newsletter

United States Hispanic Chamber of Commerce
2000 M St. NW, Suite 860
Washington, DC 20036-3307
Phone: 202-862-3939
Fax: 816-756-0575
Reports on the activities of the chamber. Highlights business opportunities for Hispanic entrepreneurs.

**Organization of
Black Designers**
300 M St. SW, Suite N110
Washington, DC 20024-4019
Phone: 202-659-3918
Web site: *http://www.core77.com/OBD/*
E-mail: *OBDesign@aol.com*
Creates a community of African-

American design professionals with a chat
room and bulletin board.

**USA Hispanic & Latino
Networking, News, and Career
Resources**
Web Address: *http://www.latpro.com/coun-try/usa.htm*

INTERNET NETWORKING RESOURCES

ONLINE DISCUSSION GROUPS

The Liszt
Web site: *http://www.liszt.com*
Enables networkers to search for on-line
discussion groups in their career field by
entering a keyword.

USENET/NEWSGROUPS

Deja.com
Web site: *http://www.deja.com/usenet*
Enables you to search for Usenet and
other discussion groups in your career
field by entering a keyword.

WEB-BASED NETWORKING

Company of Friends
Web site:
http://www2.fastcompany.com/friends.html
Fast Company magazine's global readers' network. More than 10,000 business people,
thought leaders, and change agents have
signed up in more than 100 urban areas
around the world. *Fast Company* readers are
self-organizing local discussion groups,
mentoring and networking organizations,
and creative-problem-solving teams.

Corporate Alumni Inc.
Web site: *http://www.corporatealumni.com/*
Designs, manages, and hosts communities

composed of former employees of companies. The organization's mission is to make
it easy to retain goodwill, renew friend-
ships, and build on established relationships.

High School Alumni
Web site:
http://www.Highschoolalumni.com/
Includes more than 28,000 high schools
throughout the United States. Alumni of
any American high school can visit this
site and register, update information, or
search for an old classmate. This database
can be used to locate a lost friend/
acquaintance/business associate at a high
school in another region of the country.

IndustryInsite
Web site: *http://www.industryinsite.com/*
Enables users to find people on-line who
share common bonds—same career field,
same high school, same college, same current or former employers, and more. Not
only can you locate people with whom
you can network about your career, but
many members of IndustryInsite have
signed up to be mentors and/or volunteer
resume critiquers. Free service.

**Networking Assessment for
Job Seekers**
Web site: *http://donnafisher.com/ds-asses.html*
This noninteractive site enables visitors to
measure networking skills and practices.

A FOOT IN THE DOOR

Planet Alumni

Web site: *http://www.planetalumni.com/*
A Web site committed to establishing and maintaining contact among graduating students, former classmates and other alumni of high schools, universities, and Greek organizations. Free to users.

Sixdegrees

Web site: *http://www.sixdegrees.com/*
Inspired by the theory of six degrees of separation, Sixdegrees is a personal on-line community where users have the ability to interact, communicate, and share information and experiences with millions of other members from around the world, all of whom are connected. Each person you list then adds the people they know, building connected communities. You can then use special "sixdegrees" tools to stay involved with existing friends and contacts and build new relationships with members you'd like to get to know.

CHAT ROOMS/ICQ

America Online is the best-known portal for chat rooms and instant messaging, but there are lots of other chat venues on the Internet. The best way to find out everything you need to know about chatting and even download the software you need for it is to go to CNET at *http://home. cnet.com/*. CNET even gives its top five recommendations for chat formats.

FREE HOSTING FOR WEB SITES

A number of portal sites on the Internet, such as Geocities, will host Web pages. As described on page 75, a Web page of your own can be a helpful networking tool. For a search engine that enables you to find Web sites with free Web space hosting, go to FreeWebspace.Net at *http://www.freewebspace.net/search/advanced.shtml.*

Resources

PRINT AND INTERNET NETWORKING PUBLICATIONS

Bolles, Richard Nelson. *What Color Is Your Parachute? 2000: A Practical Manual for Job-Hunters & Career-Changers.* Berkeley, California: Ten Speed Press, 1999.

CareerLab Web site:
http://www.careerlab.com/
Frank's CareerLab consulting firm advises career, outplacement, and human resources consulting and provides career management and job-search advice for senior executives and top-tier professionals. The CareerLab Web site contains several excellent networking articles.

Hansen, Katharine and Randall Hansen. *Dynamic Cover Letters: How to Sell Yourself to an Employer by Writing a Letter That Will Get Your Resume Read, Get You an Interview, and Get You the Job.* Berkeley, California: Ten Speed Press, 1995.

Hansen, Katharine. *Dynamic Cover Letters for New Graduates.* Berkeley, California: Ten Speed Press, 1998.

Krueger, Brian D. *College Grad Job Hunter: Insider Techniques and Tactics for Finding a Top-Paying Entry-Level Job.* Holbrook, Massachusetts: Adams Media Corporation, 4th edition, March 1998.

MacKay, Harvey. *Dig Your Well Before You're Thirsty: The Only Networking Book You'll Ever Need.* New York: Doubleday, 1999.

Matthews, Christopher. *Hardball.* New York: Touchstone Books, 1999.

The Office Professional. A publication of Professional Training Associates in Round Rock, Texas, and one of a set of newsletters that are only available together.

Readers subscribe to the print newsletter, *The Office Professional*, for $48 a year (in the United States; it costs a bit more elsewhere) and, if they have an e-mail address, they also receive *The Inter@ctive Office Professional* biweekly and *This Very Week*, a weekly two-page motivational newsletter. Trial subscriptions are available through Jeanne Bleil, editor of *The Inter@ctive Office Professional*. E-mail *jbleil@ncinter.net* or the publisher, Dennis Murphy, at *demwit@hardatwork.com*. Professional Training Associates also offers a Web site, *http://www.hardatwork.com* with a wealth of material for office workers of all kinds.

Rich, Jason R. *Job Hunting for the Utterly Confused*. New York: McGraw-Hill, 1998.

Whitcomb, Susan Britton. *Resume Magic: Trade Secrets of a Professional Resume Writer*. Indianapolis: Jist Works, 1998.

These last four resources would seem to be especially for African Americans, but they are excellent resources for all networkers.

Fraser, George and Les Brown. *Success Runs in Our Race: The Complete Guide to Effective Networking in the African-American Community*. New York: Avon Books, 1996.

Fraser, George. *Race for Success: The Ten Best Business Opportunities for Blacks in America*. New York: Avon Books, 1999.

(See also George Fraser's Web site: *http://www.frasernet.com/*.)

Black Enterprise magazine. Consistently offers abundant networking ideas and articles. To subscribe, go to *http://www.black-enterprise.com/* or call 800-727-7777.

Index